Differentiating Instruction With Menus

for the Inclusive Classroom

Social Studies

LOWER & ON-LEVEL MENUS
GRADES 6–8

Differentiating Instruction With Menus

for the Inclusive Classroom

Social Studies

Laurie E. Westphal

PRUFROCK PRESS INC.
WACO, TEXAS

Library of Congress Cataloging-in-Publication Data

Westphal, Laurie E., 1967-
  Differentiating instruction with menus for the inclusive classroom. Social studies, grades 6-8 / by Laurie E. Westphal.
    pages cm
Includes bibliographical references.
  ISBN 978-1-59363-966-2 (pbk.)
  1. Social sciences--Study and teaching (Elementary) 2. Social sciences--Study and teaching (Middle school) 3. Individualized instruction.
4. Inclusive education. 5. Mixed ability grouping in education. I. Title.
  LB1584.W483 2013
  372.83044--dc23
                                      2012027455

Edited by Sean Redmond

Production design by Raquel Trevino

ISBN-13: 978-1-59363-966-2

At the time of this book's publication, all facts and figures cited are the most current available; all telephone numbers, addresses, and website URLs are accurate and active; all publications, organizations, websites, and other resources exist as described in this book; and all have been verified. The author and Prufrock Press make no warranty or guarantee concerning the information and materials given out by organizations or content found at websites, and we are not responsible for any changes that occur after this book's publication. If you find an error or believe that a resource listed here is not as described, please contact Prufrock Press.

Prufrock Press Inc.
P.O. Box 8813
Waco, TX 76714-8813
Phone: (800) 998-2208
Fax: (800) 240-0333
http://www.prufrock.com

Contents

Author's Note

If you are familiar with books on various differentiation strategies, then you probably know about my Differentiating Instruction With Menus series, and you may be wondering about the differences between that series and this one, the Differentiating Instruction With Menus for the Inclusive Classroom series. In fact, when we first discussed creating this series, my editor asked how we could avoid having one series "cannibalize" (graphic, but a great word!) the other. Well, here is how I envision the two series being used:

These two series stand on their own if:
- You teach mostly lower ability, on-level, and ESL students and would like to modify your lessons on your own to accommodate a few advanced students. In this case, use this series, Differentiating Instruction With Menus for the Inclusive Classroom.
- You teach mostly advanced and high-ability students and would like to modify your lessons on your own to accommodate a few lower level students. In this case, use the Differentiating Instruction With Menus series.

These two series can serve as companions to one another if:
- You teach students with a wide range of abilities (from special education to gifted) and would benefit from having a total of three menus for a given topic of study: those for lower ability and on-level students (provided by this series, Differentiating Instruction With Menus for the Inclusive Classroom) and those for high-ability students (provided by the Differentiating Instruction With Menus series).

The menu designs used in this book reflect a successful modification technique I began using in my own classroom as the range of my students' ability levels widened. I experimented with many ways to use menus, from having students of all ability levels using the same menu with the same expectations, to having everyone using the same menu with modified contracted expectations, to using leveled menus where each student received one of three menus with some overlapping activities based on readiness, abilities, or preassessment results. I found that if the students in a given classroom had similar ability levels, I could use one menu with every student with slight modifications; however, the greater the span of ability levels, the more I needed the different leveled menus to reach everyone. Each book in the Differentiating Instruction With Menus for the Inclusive Classroom series has two leveled menus for the objectives covered: a lower level menu indicated by a ▲ and an on-level menu indicated by a ●. This way, teachers can provide more options to students with diverse abilities in the inclusive classroom. If used with the corresponding book in the Differentiating Instruction With Menus series, the teacher has a total of three leveled menus to work with.

Many teachers have told me how helpful the original Differentiating Instruction With Menus books are and how they have modified the books' menus to meet the needs of their lower level students. Teachers are always the first to make adjustments and find solutions, but wouldn't it be great if they had these preparations and changes already made for them? This is the purpose of the Differentiating Instruction With Menus for the Inclusive Classroom series.

—Laurie E. Westphal

CHAPTER 1

Choice in the Inclusive Middle School Classroom

> "When it comes to my sixth-grade math classroom, who *isn't* my audience?"
>
> *—Sixth-grade teacher, when asked to describe her target audience during a menu-writing session*

Let's begin by addressing the concept of the inclusive classroom. The term inclusive (vs. exclusive) leads one to believe that we are discussing a situation in which all students are included. In the simplest of terms, that is exactly what we are referring to as an inclusive classroom: a classroom that may have special needs students, on-level students, bilingual or ESL students, and gifted students. Although the concept is a simple one, the considerations are significant.

When thinking about the inclusive classroom and its unique ambiance, one must first consider the needs of the range of students within the classroom. Mercer, Lane, Jordan, Allsopp, and Eisele (1996) stated it best in their assessment of the needs in an inclusive classroom:

Students who are academically gifted, those who have had abundant experiences, and those who have demonstrated proficiency with lesson content typically tend to perform well when instruction is anchored at the "implicit" end of the instructional continuum. In contrast, low-performing students (i.e., students at risk for school failure, students with learning disabilities, and students with other special needs) and students with limited experience or proficiency with lesson content are most successful when instruction is explicit. Students with average academic performance tend to benefit most from the use of a variety of instructional methods that address individual needs. Instructional decisions for most students, therefore, should be based on assessment of individual needs. (pp. 230–231)

Acknowledging these varied and often contradictory needs that arise within an inclusive classroom can lead to frustration when trying to make one assignment or task fit everyone's needs. There are few—if any—traditional, teacher-directed lessons that can be implicit, explicit, and based on individual needs all at the same time. There is, however, one technique that tries to accomplish this: choice.

Choice: The Superman of Techniques in the Inclusive Middle School Classroom?

> ## "I like being able to choose. I can pick what I am good at!"
> —*Eighth-grade social studies student*

Can the offering of appropriate choices really be the hero of the inclusive middle school classroom? Can it leap buildings in a single bound and meet the needs of our implicit, explicit, and individual interests? Yes. By considering the use and benefits of choice, we can see that by offering choices, teachers really can meet the needs of the whole range of students in an inclusive classroom. Ask adults whether they would prefer to choose what to do or be told what to do, and of course, they will say they would prefer to have a choice. Students have the same feelings. Although they may not be experienced in making choices, they will make choices based on their needs, just as adults do—which makes everyone involved in the inclusive experience a little less stressed and frustrated.

Why Is Choice Essential to Middle School Students?

> "Almost every kid my age wants to be able to choose what they want to work on. They just do."
>
> —Eighth-grade math student, when asked if he thought choice was important in his classes

When considering the appropriateness of choice for middle school students, no matter their ability level, we begin by considering who (or what) our middle school students personify. During their years in middle school, adolescents struggle to determine who they are and how they fit into the world around them. They constantly try new ideas (that peroxide in the hair sounded like a good idea at the time!), new experiences (if you sit on the second-floor roof of your home one more time, I will tell your parents!), and a constant flux of personalities (preppy one day, dark nails and lipstick the next) in order to find themselves. During this process, which can take anywhere from a few months to a few years, depending on the child, children don't always have academics at the forefront of their minds. Thus, instruction and products have to engage the individuals whom these students are trying to become.

The Benefits of Choice

> "I am different in the way I do stuff. I like to build stuff with my hands."
>
> —Sixth-grade student, when asked why he enjoyed activities that allow choice

One benefit of choice is a greater sense of independence for the students, including some who have not had the opportunity to think about their own learning in the past. What a powerful feeling! Students will be designing and creating products based on what they envision, rather than what their teacher envisions. There is a possibility for more than one "right" product; all students can make products their own, no matter their level of ability. When students would enter my middle school classroom, they had often been trained by previous teachers to produce exactly what the teacher wanted, not what the students thought would be best. Teaching my students that what they envisioned could be correct (and wonderful) was often a struggle. "Is this what you want?" and "Is this right?" were popular questions as we started the school year. Allowing students to have choices in the products they create to demonstrate their learning helps create independence at any age, within any ability level.

> ## "[Choice] puts me in a good mood to participate!"
> *−Seventh-grade student*

Middle school students already have started transitioning from an academic focus to more of a social one. Choice is a way to help bring their focus back to the more desired (at least from everyone else's point of view) academic aspect of school. When students have choices in the activities they wish to complete, they are more focused on the learning that leads to their chosen products. Students become excited when they learn information that can help them develop a product they would like to create. Students pay close attention to instruction and have an immediate application for the knowledge being presented in class. Also, if students are focused, they are less likely to be off task during instruction.

The final benefit (although I am sure there are many more) is the simple fact that by offering varied choices at appropriate levels, you can address implicit instructional options, explicit instructional options, and individual needs without anyone getting overly frustrated or overworked. Many a great educator has referred to the idea that the best learning takes place when the students have a desire to learn and can feel successful while doing it. Some middle school students still have a desire to learn anything that is new to them, but many others do not want to learn anything unless it is of interest to them. By choosing from different activities according to their interests and readiness, students stretch beyond what they already know, and by offering such choices, teachers create a void that needs to be filled. This void leads to a desire to learn.

A Point to Ponder: Making Good Choices Is a Skill

> ## "It's a good point. How can we expect children to make good choices when they haven't had the chance to make any yet?"
>
> *— Eighth-grade teacher, after hearing me discuss choice as a skill*

When we think of making a good choice as a skill, much like writing an effective paragraph, it becomes easy enough to understand the processes needed to encourage students to make their own choices. In keeping with this analogy, students could certainly figure out how to write on their own, and perhaps even how to compose sentences and paragraphs, by modeling other examples. Imagine, however, the progress and strength of the writing produced when students are given guidance and even the most basic of instructions on how to accomplish the task. The written piece is still their own, but the quality of the finished piece is much stronger when guidance is given during the process. The same is true with the quality of choices students can make in the classroom.

As with writing, students—especially those with special needs—could make choices on their own, but when the teacher provides background knowledge and assistance, the choices become more meaningful and the products richer. Although all students certainly need guidance, on-level and special needs students often will need the most guidance; they have usually not been in an educational setting that has allowed them to experience different products, and the idea of choice can be new to them. Some students may have experienced only basic instructional choices, like choosing between two journal prompts or perhaps having the option of making either a poster or a PowerPoint presentation about the content being studied. Some may not have experienced even this level of choice. This lack of experience may cause frustration for both teacher and student.

Teaching Choices as a Skill

So, what is the best way to provide guidance and enable middle school students to develop the skill of making good choices? First, identify the appropriate number of choices for your students. Although the goal might be to have students choose from 20 different options, teachers might start by having their students select from a smaller number of predetermined choices the first day (if they were using a Game Show menu, for instance, students might choose one activity from the first column). Then, after that product had been created, students could choose from another set of options a few days later, and perhaps from another set the following week. By breaking students' choices down, teachers reinforce how to approach or attack a more complex and/or varied choice format in the future. All students can work up to making complex choices from longer lists of options as their choice skill level increases.

Second, although our middle school students feel they know everything, they may still need guidance on how to select the option that is right for them (and not select something just because their friends select it!). They may not automatically gravitate toward options without an exciting and detailed description of each choice. For the most part, students have been trained to produce what the teacher requests, which means that when given a choice, they will usually choose what seems to be the easiest and what the teacher most wants (then they can get to what they would prefer to be doing). This means that when the teacher discusses the different menu options, he or she has to be equally as excited about each option. The discussion of the different choices has to be animated and specific. For example, if the content is all very similar, the focus should be on the product: "If you want to do some singing, then this one is for you!" or "If you want to write and draw, then check this one as a maybe!" Sometimes, options may differ based on both content and product, in which case both can be pointed out to students to assist them in making good choices for themselves. "You have some different choices in our ecosystems unit. If you want to do something with animals and the computer, then check this one as a maybe. If you are thinking you want to do something with specimen collecting and making an exhibit, then this one might be for you." The more exposure students have to the processing the teacher provides, the more skilled they become at making good choices.

How Can Teachers Provide Choices?

> "I was concerned at first that my students would be confused by so many options and that their focus and behavior might be impacted. Instead, they really responded well—I am going to encourage other teachers to use menus for choice."
>
> *—Middle school inclusion teacher, when asked how her students with special needs responded to having choices*

When people go to a restaurant, the common goal is to find something on the menu to satisfy their hunger. Students come into our classrooms having a hunger, as well—a hunger for learning. Choice menus are a way of allowing our students to choose how they would like to satisfy that hunger. At the very least, a menu is a list of choices that students use to choose an activity (or activities) they would like to complete to show what they have learned. At best, it is a complex system in which students earn points by making choices from different areas of study. All menus should also incorporate a free-choice option for those "picky eaters" who would like to make a special order to satisfy their learning hunger.

The next few sections provide examples of the main types of menus that will be used in this book. Each menu has its own benefits, limitations or drawbacks, and time considerations. An explanation of the free-choice option and its management will follow the information on each type of menu.

Meal Menu

> "My students appreciate and need choices. At first, they may need fewer at a time."
>
> *—Middle school inclusion teacher, when asked about her students with special needs having choices*

Description

The Meal menu (see Figure 1.1) is a menu with a total of at least nine predetermined choices as well as two or more enrichment options for students. The choices are created at the various levels of Bloom's Revised taxonomy (Anderson & Krathwohl, 2001) and incorporate different learning styles, with the levels getting progressively higher as students move from breakfast to lunch and then on to dinner. All products carry the same weight for grading and have similar expectations for completion time and effort. The enrichment (dessert) options can be used for extra credit or can replace another meal option at the teacher's discretion.

Figure 1.1. Meal menu.

Benefits

User friendliness. This menu is very straightforward and easy to understand for students with special needs.

Flexibility. This menu can cover either one topic in depth or three different objectives, with each meal representing a different objective. With this menu, students have the option of completing three products: one from each meal.

Optional enrichment. Although the dessert category is not required, this part of the Meal menu allows students to have the option of going further or deeper if time permits.

Easily broken down. The Meal menu is very easy to break apart into smaller pieces for students who need support in making choices. Students could be asked to select a breakfast option while the rest of the menu is put on hold; then, once the breakfast product is submitted, they could select a lunch option, and so on.

Friendly design. Students quickly understand how to use this menu because of its real-world application.

Weighting. All products are equally weighted, so recording grades and maintaining paperwork are easily accomplished with this menu.

Short time period. This menu is intended for shorter periods of time, between 1–3 weeks.

Limitations

Few topics. This menu only covers one or three topics.

Time Considerations

This menu is usually intended for shorter periods of completion time—at most, it should take 3 weeks. If the menu focuses on one topic in depth, then it can be completed in one week.

Tic-Tac-Toe Menu

> "[Tic-Tac-Toe menus] can be a real pain. A lot of times I only liked two of the choices and had to do the last one. Usually I got stuck with a play or a presentation."
>
> —*Sixth-grade math student, when asked to step out of her comfort zone based on the tic-tac-toe design*

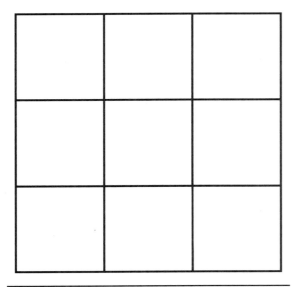

Figure 1.2. Tic-Tac-Toe menu.

Description

The Tic-Tac-Toe menu (see Figure 1.2) is a well-known, commonly used menu that contains a total of eight predetermined choices and, if appropriate, one free choice for students. Choices can be created at the same level of Bloom's Revised taxonomy or can be arranged in such a way to allow for three different levels or content areas. If all choices have been created at the same level of

Bloom's Revised taxonomy, then each choice has similar expectations for completion time and effort.

Benefits

Flexibility. This menu can cover either one topic in depth or three different topics, objectives, or even content areas. When this menu covers just one objective and all tasks are from the same level of Bloom's Revised taxonomy, students have the option of completing three projects in a tic-tac-toe pattern, or simply picking three from the menu. When the menu covers three objectives or different levels of Bloom's Revised taxonomy, students will need to complete a tic-tac-toe pattern (either a vertical column or horizontal row) to be sure they have completed one activity from each objective or level.

Stretching. When students make choices on this menu, completing a row or column based on its design, they will usually face one choice that is out of their comfort zone, be it for its Bloom's Revised taxonomy level, its product learning style, or its content. They will complete this "uncomfortable" choice because they want to do the other two in that row or column.

Friendly design. Students quickly understand how to use this menu. It is nonthreatening because it does not contain points, and therefore it seems to encourage students to stretch out of their comfort zones.

Weighting. All projects are equally weighted, so recording grades and maintaining paperwork is easily accomplished with this menu.

Short time period. This menu is intended for shorter periods of time, between 1–3 weeks.

Limitations

Few topics. This menu only covers one or three topics.

Student compromise. Although this menu does allow choice, a student will sometimes have to compromise and complete an activity he or she would not have chosen because it completes the required tic-tac-toe. (This is not always bad, though!)

Time Considerations

This menu is usually intended for shorter amounts of completion time—at the most, it should take 3 weeks with one product submitted each week. If the menu focuses on one topic in depth, it can be completed in one week.

List Menu

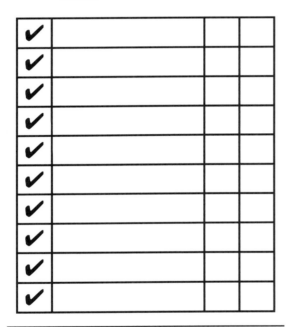

Figure 1.3. List menu.

Description

The List menu (see Figure 1.3), or Challenge List, is a more complex menu than the Tic-Tac-Toe menu, with a total of at least 10 predetermined choices, each with its own point value, and at least one free choice for students. Choices are simply listed with assigned points based on the levels of Bloom's Revised taxonomy. The choices carry different weights and have different expectations for completion time and effort. A point criterion is set forth that equals 100%, and students choose how they wish to attain that point goal.

Benefits

Responsibility. Students have complete control over their grades. They really like the idea that they can guarantee their grades if they complete the required work. If they lose points on one of the chosen assignments, then they can complete another to be sure they have met their goal points. This responsibility over their own grades also allows a shift in thinking about grades: whereas many students think of grades in terms of how the teacher judged their work, having control over their grades leads students to understand that they earn them.

Different learning levels. This menu also has the flexibility to allow for individualized contracts for different learning levels within the classroom. Each student can choose what products will provide the points for his or her 100%.

Concept reinforcement. This menu allows for an in-depth study of material; however, with the different levels of Bloom's Revised taxonomy being represented, students who are still learning the concepts can choose some of the lower level point value projects to reinforce the basics before jumping into the higher level activities.

Variety. A List menu offers a larger variety of product choices. There is guaranteed to be a product of interest to everyone.

Limitations

One topic. This menu is best used for one topic in depth, so that students don't miss any specific content.

Cannot guarantee objectives. If this menu is used for more than one topic, it is possible for a student to not complete an activity for each objective, depending on the choices he or she makes.

Preparation. Teachers need to have all materials ready at the beginning of the unit for students to be able to choose any of the activities on the list, which requires advanced planning. (Note: Once the materials are assembled, the menu is wonderfully low stress!)

Time Considerations

This menu is usually intended for shorter amounts of completion time—at the most, 2 weeks.

20-50-80 Menu

> "My least favorite menu is 20-50-80. You can't just do the easy ones. If you pick a 20, then you have to do an 80. No matter what, you have to do one of the hard ones."
>
> *—Seventh-grade student*

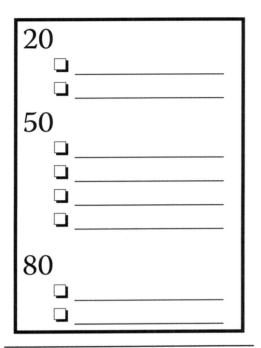

20

☐ _____
☐ _____

50

☐ _____
☐ _____
☐ _____
☐ _____

80

☐ _____
☐ _____

Figure 1.4. 20-50-80 menu.

Description

A 20-50-80 menu (see Figure 1.4) is a variation on a List menu, with a total of at least eight predetermined choices: two choices with a point value of 20, at least four choices with a point value of 50, and at least two choices with a point value of 80. Choices are assigned points based on the levels of Bloom's Revised taxonomy. Choices with a point value of 20 represent the "remember" and "understand" levels, choices with a point value of 50 represent the "apply" and "analyze" levels, and choices with a point value of 80 represent the "evaluate" and "create" levels. All levels of choices carry different weights and have different expectations for completion time and effort. Students are expected to earn 100 points for a 100%. Students choose what combination they would like to use to attain that point goal.

Benefits

Responsibility. With this menu, students still have complete control over their grades.

Guaranteed activity. This menu's design is also set up in such a way that students must complete at least one activity at a higher level of Bloom's Revised taxonomy in order to reach their point goal.

Great introductory menu. This menu is one of the shortest menus; if students choose well, they can accomplish their goal by completing only two products. This menu is usually less daunting than some of the longer, more complex menus. It provides students a great introduction to the process of making choices.

Limitations

One topic. Although it can be used for more than one topic, this menu works best with an in-depth study of one topic.

Higher level thinking. Students may choose to complete only one activity at a higher level of thinking.

Time Considerations

This menu is usually intended for a shorter amount of completion time—at the most, one week.

Baseball Menu

> ### "There were so many choices, and most of them were fun activities!"
>
> *—Sixth-grade student*

Description

The Baseball menu (see Figure 1.5) is a baseball-based variation of the List menu with a total of at least 20 predetermined choices: choices are given values as singles, doubles, triples, or home runs based on the levels of Bloom's Revised taxonomy. Singles represent the remember and understand levels; doubles, the apply and analyze levels; triples, the evaluate level; and home runs, the create level. All levels of choices carry different weights and have different expectations for completion time and effort. Students are expected to earn a certain number of runs (around all four bases) for a 100%. Students choose what combination they would like to use to attain that number of runs.

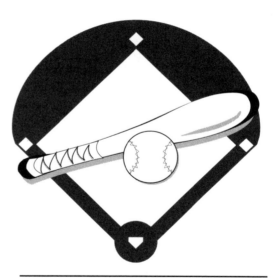

Figure 1.5. Baseball menu.

Benefits

Responsibility. With this menu, students still have complete control over their own grades.

Flexibility and variety. This menu allows for many choices at each level. Students should have no trouble finding something that catches their interest.

Theme. This menu has a fun theme that students enjoy and can be used throughout the classroom. A bulletin board can be set up with a baseball diamond, with each student having his or her own player who can move through the bases. Not only can students keep track of their own RBIs, but they can also have a visual reminder of what they have completed.

Limitations

One topic. This menu is best used for one all-encompassing unit with many objectives for in-depth study.

Preparation. With so many choices available to students, teachers should have all materials ready at the beginning of the unit for students to be able to choose any of the activities on the list. This sometimes causes a consideration for space in the classroom.

Time Considerations

This menu is usually intended for a longer amount of completion time, depending on the number of runs required for a 100%—at the most, 4 or 5 weeks.

Game Show Menu

"This menu was very easy to break down for my [students needing modifications], as we could focus on just one column at a time. They were very successful with the format."

—Seventh-grade science teacher

Description

The Game Show menu (see Figure 1.6) is a complex menu. It covers multiple topics or objectives with at least three predetermined choices and a free-choice option for each objective. Choices are assigned points based on the levels of Bloom's Revised taxonomy. All choices carry different weights and have different expectations for completion time and effort. A point criterion is set forth that equals 100%. Students must complete at least one activity from each objective in order to reach their goal.

Benefits

Figure 1.6. Game Show menu.

Free choice. This menu allows many choices for students, but if they do not want to complete the offered activities, they can propose their own activity for each objective.

Responsibility. This menu allows students to guarantee their own grades.

Different learning levels. This menu has the flexibility to allow for individualized contracts for different learning levels within the classroom. Each student can contract for a certain number of points for his or her 100%.

Objectives guaranteed. The teacher is guaranteed that the students complete an activity from each objective covered, even if it is at a lower level.

Limitations

Confirm expectations. The only real limitation for this menu is that students (and parents) must understand the guidelines for completing the menu.

Time Considerations

This menu is usually intended for a longer amount of completion time. Although it can be used as a yearlong menu (each column could be for one grading period), it is usually intended for 2–3 weeks.

Free Choice in the Inclusive Classroom

> "I didn't do one [free choice] on the menu. I didn't really get it, but I saw a poster [as a free choice] that my friend did that was really cool. I think I want to do a free choice on the next one."
>
> —*Seventh-grade inclusion student*

Most of the menus included in this book allow students to submit a free-choice product. This is a product of their choosing that addresses the content being studied and shows what the student has learned about the topic. Although this option is available, students may not fully understand its benefits or immediately respond to the opportunity even after it has been explained. In the past, certain students may have been offered choices and enjoyed the idea of taking charge of their own learning; however, students with special needs may not have had much exposure to this concept. Their educational experiences tend to be objective-based and teacher-driven. This is not to say that they would not respond well to the idea of free choice; in fact, they can embrace it as enthusiastically as gifted students can. The most significant difference between these two groups successfully approaching free choice is the amount of content needed by the student before he or she embarks on a proposed option. Students with special needs need to feel confident in their knowledge of the content and information before they are ready to step out on their own, propose their own ideas, and create their own products. Gifted students may be comfortable with less knowledge and structure.

With most of the menus, the students are allowed to submit a free-choice product for their teacher's consideration. Figure 1.7 shows two sample proposal forms that have been used successfully in my classroom. With middle school students, this cuts down greatly on the whining that often accompanies any task given to students. A copy of these forms should be given to each student when the menu is first introduced. The form used is based on the type of menu being presented. For example, if you are using the Tic-Tac-Toe menu, there is no need to submit a point proposal. A discussion should be held with the students so they understand the expectations of a free choice. I always had a few students who

Name: _____   Teacher's Approval: _____

Free-Choice Proposal Form for Point-Based Menu

Points Requested: _____   Points Approved: _____

Proposal Outline

1. What specific topic or idea will you learn about?

2. What criteria should be used to grade it? (Neatness, content, creativity, artistic value, etc.)

3. What will your product look like?

4. What materials will you need from the teacher to create this product?

Name: _____   Teacher's Approval: _____

Free-Choice Proposal Form

Proposal Outline

1. What specific topic or idea will you learn about?

2. What criteria should be used to grade it? (Neatness, content, creativity, artistic value, etc.)

3. What will your product look like?

4. What materials will you need from the teacher to create this product?

Figure 1.7. Sample proposal forms for free choice.

did not want to complete a task on the menu; students are welcome to create their own free-choice proposals and submit them for approval. The biggest complainers will not always go to the trouble to complete the form and have it approved, but it is their choice not to do so. The more free choice is used and encouraged, the more students will begin to request it. How the students show their knowledge will begin to shift from teacher-focused to student-designed activities. If students do not want to make a proposal using the proposal form after the teacher has discussed the entire menu and its activities, then they can place the unused form in a designated place in the classroom. Others may want to use their forms, and it is often surprising who wants to submit a proposal form after hearing about the opportunity!

Proposal forms must be submitted before students begin working on their free-choice products. The teacher then knows what the students are working on, and the student knows the expectations the teacher has for that product. Once the project has been approved, the form can easily be stapled to the student's menu sheet. The student can refer to the form while developing the free-choice product, and when the grading takes place, the teacher can refer to the agreement for the graded features of the product.

Each part of the proposal form is important and needs to be discussed with students:

- *Name/Teacher's Approval.* The student must submit this form to the teacher for approval. The teacher will carefully review all of the information, discuss any suggestions or alterations with the student, if needed, and then sign the top.
- *Points Requested.* Found only on the point-based menu proposal form, this is where negotiation may need to take place. Students usually will submit their first request for a very high number (even the 100% goal). They tend to equate the amount of time something will take with the number of points it should earn. But please note that the points are always based on the levels of Bloom's Revised taxonomy. For example, a PowerPoint presentation with a vocabulary word quiz would get minimal points, although it may have taken a long time to create. If the students have not been exposed to the levels of Bloom's Revised taxonomy, this can be difficult to explain. You can always refer to the popular "Bloom's Verbs" to help explain the difference between time-consuming and higher level activities.

- *Points Approved.* Found only on the point-based menu proposal form, this is the final decision recorded by the teacher once the point haggling is finished.
- *Proposal Outline.* This is where the student will tell you everything about the product he or she intends to complete. These questions should be completed in such a way that you can really picture what the student is planning to complete. This also shows you that the student knows what he or she plans to complete.
  - *What specific topic or idea will you learn about?* Students need to be specific here. It is not acceptable to write "science" or "reading." This is where students look at the objectives of the lesson and choose which objective their product demonstrates.
  - *What criteria should be used to grade it?* Although there are rubrics for all of the products that the students might create, it is important for the students to explain what criteria are most important to evaluate the product. The student may indicate that the rubric being used for all of the predetermined products is fine; however, he or she may also want to add other criteria here.
  - *What will your product look like?* It is important that this response be as detailed as possible. If a student cannot express what it will look like, then he or she has probably not given the free-choice plan enough thought.
  - *What materials will you need from the teacher to create this product?* This is an important consideration. Sometimes students do not have the means to purchase items for their project. This can be negotiated as well, but if you ask what students may need, they will often develop even grander ideas for their free choice.

CHAPTER 2

How to Use Menus in the Inclusive Classroom

There are different ways to use instructional menus in the inclusive classroom. In order to decide how to implement each menu, the following questions should be considered: How much prior knowledge of the topic being taught do the students have before the unit or lesson begins, how confident are your students in making choices and working independently, and how much intellectually appropriate information is readily available for students to obtain on their own? After considering these questions, there are a variety of ways to use menus in the classroom.

Building Background Knowledge

> "I have students with so many different experiences—sometimes I spend a lot more time than I allotted to review and get everyone up to speed before we get started."
>
> —Seventh-grade social studies teacher

There are many ways to use menus in the classroom. One way that is often overlooked is using menus to review or build background knowledge before a unit begins. This is frequently used when students have had exposure to upcoming content in the past, perhaps during the previous year's instruction or through similar life experiences. In reality, most middle school students have had exposure to the basic information needed in their classes; however, students may not remember the details of the content well enough to proceed with the upcoming unit immediately. A shorter menu covering the background or previous year's objectives can be provided in the weeks prior to the new unit so that students have the opportunity to recall and engage with the information in a meaningful way. They will then be ready to take their knowledge to a deeper level during the unit. For example, 2 weeks before starting a unit on the Revolutionary War, the teacher may select a short menu on the famous people of the time period and the events leading up to the war, knowing that the students have covered the content in the past and should be able to successfully work independently on the menu by engaging their prior knowledge. Students work on products from the menu as anchor activities and homework throughout the 2 weeks preceding the Revolutionary War unit, with all products being submitted prior to the unit's initiation. This way, the students have been in the "revolutionary frame of mind" independently for 2 weeks and are ready to investigate the topic further.

Enrichment and Supplemental Activities

> "I wanted to start allowing some choice in my novel projects, so I chose a menu that matched each genre. It really worked well—the students worked on their projects every day when they had time."
>
> *—Sixth-grade language arts teacher*

Using the menus for enrichment and supplementary activities is the most common way of using menus. In this case, the students usually do not have a lot of background knowledge, and information about the topic may not be readily available to all students. The teacher will introduce the menu and the activities at the beginning of a unit. The teacher then will progress through the content at the normal rate using his or her curricular materials, periodically allowing class and homework time throughout the unit for students to work on their menu choices to supplement a deeper understanding of the lessons being taught. This method is very effective, as it incorporates an immediate use for the content the teacher is covering. For example, at the beginning of a unit on Aztec culture, the teacher may introduce the menu with the explanation that students may not yet have all of the knowledge needed to complete their choices. During the unit, however, more content will be provided, and the students will be prepared to work on new choices. If students want to work ahead, they can certainly find the information on their own, but that is not required. Although some students often see this as a challenge and will begin to investigate concepts mentioned in the menu before the teacher has discussed them, other students begin to develop questions about the concepts and are ready to ask them when the teacher covers the material. This helps build an immense pool of background knowledge and possible content questions before the topic is even discussed in the classroom. As teachers, we constantly fight the battle of trying to get students to read ahead or come to class already prepared for discussion. By introducing a menu at the beginning of a unit and allowing students to complete products as instruction progresses, we encourage the students to naturally investigate the information and come to class prepared without having to make preparation a separate requirement.

Mainstream Instructional Activities

> "On your suggestion, I tried using the Game Show menu with my geometry unit because I had 3 days of instruction that the students knew well and could work on independently. They really responded to the independence."
>
> *—Eighth-grade math teacher*

Another option for using menus in the classroom is to replace certain curricular activities the teacher uses to teach the specified content. In this case, the students may have some limited background knowledge about the content and have information readily available for them among their classroom resources. This situation allows the teacher to pick and choose which aspects of the content need to be directly taught to the students in large or small groups and which can be appropriately learned and reinforced through product menus. The unit is then designed using formal instructional large-group lessons, smaller informal group lessons, and specific menu days during which the students use the menu to reinforce their prior knowledge. In order for this option to be effective, the teacher must feel very comfortable with the students' prior knowledge level and their readiness to work independently. Another variation on this method is using the menus to drive station activities. Stations have many different functions in the middle school classroom. They can contain activities that are best completed individually to reinforce the content being taught, or—a more common occurrence in middle school—they can allow students access to products or activities that may include specialized resources. Many classrooms may not have enough supplies or resources to set up eight versions of the same activity; however, by making different "resource-heavy" activities available at stations, students can experience the content while the teacher may only need one set-up of each activity.

Mini-Lessons

> "I have so many different levels in my classroom, using menus with mini-lessons has been a life saver. I can actually work with small groups, and everyone else doesn't run wild!"
>
> *—Eighth-grade math teacher*

Yet another option for menus is to use them with mini-lessons, with the menus driving the accompanying classroom activities. This method is best used when the majority of the students have similar amounts of knowledge about the topic. The teacher can design 15–20-minute mini-lessons in which students quickly review basic concepts that are already familiar to them and are then exposed to the new content in a short and concise way. Then students are turned loose to choose an activity on the menu to show that they understand the concept. The Game Show menu usually works very well with this method of instruction, as the topics across the top usually lend themselves to these mini-lessons. It is important that the students either have some prior knowledge of the content or are effective at working independently, because the lesson cycle is shorter in this use of menus. Using menus in this way does shorten the amount of time teachers have to use the guided practice step of the lesson, so all instruction and examples should be carefully selected. By using the menus in this way, the teacher avoids the one-size-fits-all independent practice portion of the lesson. If there are still a few students struggling, they can be pulled into a small-group situation while the other students work on their choices from the menu. Another important consideration is the independence level of the students. In order for this use of menus to be effective, students will need to be able to work independently for up to 30 minutes after the mini-lesson. Because students are often interested in the product they have chosen, this is not a critical issue, but it is still one worth mentioning as teachers consider how they would like to use various menus in their classrooms.

Introducing and Using Leveled Menus With Students

"That's not fair . . ."

—A middle school student somewhere in the world, this very minute

The menus in this book are tiered versions of the menus found in its companion series, Differentiating Instruction With Menus. Although the topics and objectives are alike, these menus may have different values assigned to the same tasks, slightly different wording for similar tasks, the same product options in a menu of a different format, or even tasks that are only available on certain menus. All of these minor modifications make certain menus more appropriate for different students based on their readiness, interests, and ability levels.

As we all know, middle school students tend to compare answers, work, and ideas, and the same goes for their menu choices. Although students may notice the slight aforementioned differences, it may not be an issue when students are working in ability groups, as students are comfortable with not having the exact same options as their classmates. It may also not be an issue when the menus are presented in a matter-of-fact manner, as everyone is getting a menu that was especially chosen for him or her, so students may notice some differences between their menus. Students should rest assured that target numbers (e.g., a goal of 100 points must be met to receive a 100%) is equal for all of the menus provided, and that the activities most often preferred by students are found on all of the menus. Students should also know that most of the menus have a free-choice proposal option, so if they really want to do one of the activities found on another menu in the classroom, they are welcome to submit a free-choice proposal form in order to complete that activity. By presenting tiered menus with confidence and by making it clear that each menu is selected specifically for each student, you can make students much more willing to accept the system and proceed within the confines that you have set.

That being said, you may still have a few students who say, in that dreaded nasal, accusatory, middle schooler's tone: "That's still not fair!" When I first starting using leveled menus with my eighth graders, I heard a few comments like this. They quickly dissipated with my standard and practiced responses. Of course, the first response (which they do not always appreciate) is that fair is not the same as equal. I know students do not like to hear this response, as it is patently true and therefore difficult to dispute. Secondly, I remind students that everyone has different strengths, and the menus are distributed in order to emphasize students' strengths. Again, they know this; they just do not like to acknowledge it. Lastly, if the students are being especially surly, I sometimes have to play the "parent card," meaning that I am the teacher and therefore have the right to do what I feel is best for each student. This last option is nonnegotiable, and although students may not like it, they understand the tone and sentiment, as they have usually experienced it at home.

The bottom line when it comes to tiered menus is that students will respond to the use of different menus within a classroom based on how the teacher presents or reacts to the menus. In the past, when I have used different formats, I have addressed the format or obvious differences in a matter-of-fact manner, by saying things such as, "I have spiced things up with this menu and have three different ones that I will pass out. You may receive one that is different than your neighbor's, but whichever one you receive is going to be lots of fun for you!" Other times, when the menus are very similar in their formats and graphics, I simply distribute them and address concerns when they are brought up. For the most part, students are more likely to simply go with what they have been given when the differences in menus are presented confidently, without being open to debate or complaint.

CHAPTER 3

Guidelines for Products

> "I got to do a play! In math!"
>
> *—Seventh-grade student*

This chapter outlines the different types of products included in the featured menus, as well as the guidelines and expectations for each. It is very important that students know exactly what the expectations of a completed product are when they choose to work on it. By discussing these expectations before students begin and having the information readily available ahead of time, you will limit the frustration on everyone's part.

$1 Contract

> "The $1 contract sure cuts out those late-night trips to buy supplies for [my son's] products!"
>
> *—Sixth-grade teacher and parent of a middle schooler*

$1 Contract

I did not spend more than $1.00 on my _____.

_____   _____
Student Signature   Date

My child, _____, did not spend more than $1.00 on the product he or she created.

_____   _____
Parent Signature   Date

Figure 3.1. $1 contract.

Consideration should be given to the cost of creating the products featured on any menu. The resources available to students vary within a classroom, and students should not be graded on the amount of materials they can purchase to make a product look better. These menus are designed to equalize the resources students have available. The materials for most products are available for less than a dollar and can often be found in a teacher's classroom as part of the classroom supplies. If a product requires materials from the student, there is a $1 contract as part of the product criteria. This is a very important piece in the explanation of the product. First of all, by limiting the amount of money a child can spend, teachers create an equal amount of resources for all students. Second, this practice actually encourages a more creative product. When students are limited by the amount of materials they can readily purchase, they often have to use materials from home in new and unique ways. Figure 3.1 is a sample of the contract that has been used many times in my classroom with various products.

The Products

Table 3.1 contains a list of the products used in this book, along with ideas for other products that students may choose to develop as free-choice activities. These products were chosen for their flexibility in meet-

Table 3.1
Products

Visual	Kinesthetic	Auditory
Acrostic	Board Game	Children's Book
Advertisement	Bulletin Board Display	Commercial/Infomercial
Book Cover	Class Game	Game Show
Brochure/Pamphlet	Commercial/Infomercial	Interview
Bulletin Board Display	Concentration Cards	News Report
Cartoon/Comic Strip	Cross-Cut Diagram/Model	Oral Presentation of Created
Children's Book	Diorama	Product
Class Lesson—Written Only	Experiment	Play/Skit
Collage	Flipbook	PowerPoint—Speaker
Collection	Folded Quiz Book	Puppet
Cross-Cut Diagram/Model	Mobile	Song/Rap
Crossword Puzzle	Model	Speech
Data Table	Mural	Student-Taught Lesson
Drawing	Museum Exhibit	Video
Essay	Play/Skit	You Be the Person
Folded Quiz Book	Product Cube	Presentation
Graph	Puppet	
Graphic Novel	Quiz Board	
Greeting Card	Sculpture	
Instruction Card	Student-Taught Lesson	
Journal/Diary	Three-Dimensional Timeline	
Letter	Trophy	
Map	Video	
Mind Map		
Newspaper Article		
Paragraph		
Pie Graph		
Poster		
PowerPoint—Stand Alone		
Questionnaire		
Quiz		
Recipe Card		
Scrapbook		
Story		
Summary		
Survey		
Three Facts and a Fib		
Trading Cards		
Venn Diagram		
Video		
WebQuest		
Windowpane		
Worksheet		

ing different learning styles, as well as for being products many teachers are already using in their classrooms. They have been arranged by learning style—visual, kinesthetic, or auditory—and each menu has been designed to include products from all of these learning styles. Of course, some of the products may represent more than one style of learning, depending on how they are presented or implemented. Some of these products are featured in the menus more often than others, but students may choose the less common products as free-choice options.

Product Frustrations

One of the biggest frustrations that accompany the use of these various products on menus is the barrage of questions about the products themselves. Students can become so wrapped up in the products and the criteria for creating them that they do not focus on the content being presented. This is especially true when menus are introduced to the class. Students can spend an exorbitant amount of time asking the teacher about the products mentioned on the menu. When this happens, what should have been a 10–15-minute menu introduction turns into 45–50 minutes of discussion about product expectations. In order to facilitate the introduction of the menu products, teachers may consider showing students examples of the product(s) from the previous year. Although this can be helpful, it can also lead to additional frustration on the part of both the teacher and the students. Some students may not feel that they can produce a product as nice, as big, as special, or as (you fill in the blank) as the example, or when shown an example, students might interpret that as meaning that the teacher would like something exactly like the one he or she showed to students. To avoid this situation, I would propose that when using examples, the example students are shown be a "blank" one that demonstrates how to create only the shell of the product. If an example of a windowpane is needed, for instance, students might be shown a blank piece of paper that is divided into six panes. The students can then take the skeleton of the product and make it their own as they create their own version of the windowpane using their information.

Product Guidelines

Most frustrations associated with products can be addressed proactively through the use of standardized, predetermined product guidelines, to be shared with students prior to the creation of any products.

These product guidelines are designed in a specific yet generic way, such that any time throughout the school year that the students select a product, that product's guidelines will apply. A beneficial side effect of using set guidelines for a product is the security it creates. Students are often reticent to try something new, as doing so requires taking a risk. Traditionally, when students select a product, they ask questions about creating it, hope they remember and understood all of the details, and turn it in. It can be quite a surprise when they receive the product back and realize that it was not complete or was not what was expected. As you can imagine, students may not want to take the risk on something new the next time; they often prefer to do what they know and be successful. Through the use of product guidelines, students can begin to feel secure in their choices before they start working on new products. If they are not feeling secure, they tend to stay within their comfort zone.

The product guidelines for menu products included in this book, as well as some potential free-choice options, are presented in an easy-to-read card format (see Figure 3.2). (The guidelines for some products, such as summaries, are omitted because teachers often have their own criteria for these products.) Once the products and/or menus have been selected, there are many options available to share this information.

There really is no one right way to share the product guideline information with your students. It all depends on their abilities and needs. Some teachers choose to duplicate and distribute all of the product guidelines pages to students at the beginning of the year so that each child has his or her own copy while working on products. As another option, a few classroom sets can be created by gluing each product guideline card onto a separate index card, hole punching the corner of each card, and placing all of the cards on a metal ring. These ring sets can be placed in a central location or at stations where students can borrow and return them as they work on their products. This allows for the addition of products as they are introduced. Some teachers prefer to introduce product guidelines as students experience products on their menus. In this case, product guidelines from the menu currently assigned can be enlarged, laminated, and posted on a bulletin board for easy access during classroom work. Some teachers may choose to reproduce each menu's specific product guidelines on the back of the menu. No matter which method teachers choose to share the information with the students, they will save themselves a lot of time and frustration by having the product guidelines available for student reference (e.g., "Look at your product guidelines—I think that will answer your question").

Acrostic	Advertisement	Board Game
• Must be at least 8.5" by 11" • Neatly written or typed • Target word written down the left side of the paper • Each descriptive phrase chosen must begin with one of the letters from the target word • Each descriptive phrase chosen must be related to the target word	• Must be at least 8.5" by 11" • A slogan should be included • Color picture of item or service should be included • Include price, if appropriate • Can be created on the computer	• At least four thematic game pieces • At least 20 colored/thematic squares • At least 15 question/activity cards • Include a thematic title on the board • Include a complete set of rules for playing the game • At least the size of an open file folder
Book Cover	**Brochure/Pamphlet**	**Bulletin Board Display**
• Front cover—title, author, image • Front inside flap—paragraph summary of the book • Back inside flap—brief biography of author with at least three details • Back cover—your comments about the book • Spine—title and author	• Must be at least 8.5" by 11" • Must be in three-fold format; front fold has the title and picture • Must have both pictures and written text • Information should be in paragraph form with at least five facts included • Can be created on the computer	• Must fit within assigned space on bulletin board or wall • Must include at least five details • Must have a title • Must have at least five different elements (e.g., posters, papers, questions) • Must have at least one interactive element that engages the reader
Cartoon/Comic Strip	**Children's Book**	**Class Game**
• Must be at least 8.5" by 11" • Must have at least six cells • Must have meaningful dialogue • Must include color	• Must have a cover with book's title and student's name as author • Must have at least 10 pages • Each page should have an illustration to accompany the story • Neatly written or typed • Can be created on the computer	• Game should allow all class members to participate • Must have only a few, easy-to-understand rules • Can be a new variation on a current game • Must have multiple questions • Must provide answer key before game is played • Must be approved by teacher before being played

Figure 3.2. Product guidelines.

Class Lesson—Written Only	Collage	Collection
(Note: For a class lesson that is presented, use the student-taught lesson rubric.) • Is original—do not just print or copy an activity as is • States the objectives that will be taught • Includes at least one warm-up question • Presents the information in a clear way • Includes all of the important information • Has a way for students to practice the content • Includes a quiz or method of assessment	• Must be at least 8.5" by 11" • Pictures must be cut neatly from magazines or newspapers (no clip art from the computer or the Internet) • Label items as required in task	• Contains number of items stated in task • All items must fit in the space designated by the teacher • All items must be brought to class in a box or bag • No living things!
Commercial/Infomercial	**Concentration Cards**	**Cross-Cut Diagram/Model**
• Must be 1–2 minutes in length • Script must be turned in before the commercial is presented • Can be presented live to an audience or recorded • Should have props or some form of costume(s) • Can include more than one person	• At least 20 index cards (10 matching sets) • Both pictures and words can be used • Information should be placed on just one side of each card • Include an answer key that shows the matches • All cards must be submitted in a carrying bag	• Must include a scale to show the relationship between the diagram/model and the actual item • Must include details for each layer • If creating a diagram, must also meet the guidelines for a poster • If creating a model, must also meet the guidelines for a model
Crossword Puzzle	**Data Table**	**Diorama**
• At least 20 significant words or phrases should be included • Develop appropriate clues • Include puzzle and answer key • Can be created on the computer	• Table and data have proper units, titles, and descriptions • All data should be recorded neatly and be easy to read • If created by hand, all lines should be straight and neat	• Must be at least 4" by 5" by 8" • Must be self-standing • All interior space must be covered with relevant pictures and information • Name written on the back • Informational/title card attached to diorama • $1 contract signed

Figure 3.2. Continued.

Drawing	Essay	Experiment
• Must be at least 8.5" by 11" • Must show what is requested in the task statement • Must include color • Must be neatly drawn by hand • Must have title • Name written on the back	• Must be neatly written or typed • Must cover the specific topic in detail • Must be at least three paragraphs • Must include resources or bibliography if appropriate	• Includes a hypothesis or purpose • States specific materials for experiment • Includes detailed procedures and data • Includes a written conclusion in paragraph form • Information neatly written or typed as a report
Flipbook	**Folded Quiz Book**	**Game Show**
• Must be at least 8.5" by 11" folded in half • All information or opinions are supported by facts • Created with the correct number of flaps cut into the top • Color is optional • Name must be written on the back	• Must be at least 8.5" by 11" folded in half • Must have at least 10 questions • Created with the correct number of flaps cut into the top • Questions written or typed neatly on upper flaps • Answers written or typed neatly inside each flap • Color is optional • Name written on the back	• Needs an emcee or host • Must have at least two contestants • Must have at least one regular round and a bonus round • Questions will be content specific • Props can be used, but are not mandatory
Graph	**Graphic Novel**	**Greeting Card**
• Must have a title • Axes must be labeled with units • All data must be clearly represented • Can be created on the computer • If created by hand, must use graph paper	• Should use color • Must tell a story • Should be at least 10 pages in length • Can be created on the computer	• Front—colored pictures, words optional • Front inside—personal note related to topic • Back inside—greeting or saying; must meet product criteria • Back outside—logo, publisher, and price for card

Figure 3.2. Continued.

Instruction Card	Interview	Journal/Diary
• Must be no larger than 5" by 8" • Created on heavy paper or index card • Neatly written or typed • Uses color drawings • Provides instructions stated in the task	• Must have at least eight questions about the topic being studied • Person chosen for interview must be an "expert" and qualified to provide answers • Questions and answers must be neatly written or typed	• Neatly written or typed • Should include the appropriate number of entries • Should include a date if appropriate • Should be written in first person

Letter	Map	Mind Map
• Neatly written or typed • Uses proper letter format • At least three paragraphs in length • Must follow type of letter stated in the menu (e.g., friendly, persuasive, informational)	• Must be at least 8.5" by 11" • Accurate information is included • Includes at least 10 relevant locations • Includes compass rose, legend, scale, and key	• Must be at least 8.5" by 11" • Uses unlined paper • Must have one central idea • Follows the "no more than four" rule—no more than four words coming from any one word • Should be neatly written or developed using a computer

Mobile	Model	Mural
• Includes at least 10 pieces of related information • Includes color and pictures • At least three layers of hanging information • Hangs in a balanced way	• Must be at least 8" by 8" by 12" • Parts of model must be labeled • Should be in scale if possible • Must include a title card • Name should be permanently written on the model	• Must be at least 22" x 54" • Must contain at least five pieces of important information • Must have colored pictures • Words are optional, but a title should be included • Name should be permanently written on the back

Figure 3.2. Continued.

Museum Exhibit	News Report	Newspaper Article
• Should have title for exhibit • Must include at least five "artifacts" • Each artifact must be labeled with a neatly written card • Exhibit must fit within the size assigned • $1 contract required • No expensive or irreplaceable objects in the display	• Must address the who, what, where, when, why, and how of the topic • Script of report must be turned in with project (or before if performance will be live) • Must be either performed live or recorded	• Must be informational in nature • Must follow standard newspaper format • Must include picture with caption that supports article • At least three paragraphs in length • Neatly written or typed
Paragraph	**Pie Graph**	**Play/Skit**
• Neatly written or typed • Must have topic sentence, at least three supporting sentences or details, and a concluding sentence • Must use appropriate vocabulary and follow grammar rules	• Must have a title • Must have a label for each area or be color coded with a key • Must include the percentages for each area of the graph • Calculations must be provided if needed to create the pie graph • Should be created neatly by hand or using a computer	• Must be 4–6 minutes in length • Script must be turned in before play is presented • May be presented to an audience or recorded for future showing • Should have props or some form of costume(s) • Can include more than one person
Poster	**PowerPoint—Speaker**	**PowerPoint—Stand Alone**
• Should be the size of a standard poster board • Includes at least five pieces of important information • Must have title • Must contain both words and pictures • Name written on the back • Bibliography included as needed	• At least 10 informational slides and one title slide with student's name • No more than two words per page • Slides must have color and no more than one graphic per page • Animations are optional but should not distract from information being presented • Presentation should be timed and flow with the speech being given	• At least 10 informational slides and one title slide with student's name • No more than 10 words per page • Slides must have color and no more than one graphic per page • Animations are optional but should not distract from information being presented

Figure 3.2. Continued.

Product Cube	Puppet	Questionnaire
• All six sides of the cube must be filled with information • Neatly written or typed • Name must be printed neatly on the bottom of one of the sides • Should be submitted flat for grading	• Puppet should be handmade and must have a moveable mouth • A list of supplies used to make the puppet must be turned in with the puppet • $1 contract signed • If used in a puppet show, must also meet the criteria for a play	• Neatly written or typed • Includes at least 10 questions with possible answers, and at least one answer that requires a written response • Questions must be helpful to gathering information on the topic being studied
Quiz	**Quiz Board**	**Recipe Card**
• Must be at least a half sheet of paper long • Neatly written or typed • Must cover the specific topic in detail • Must include at least five questions including a short answer question • Must have at least one graphic • An answer key must be turned in with the quiz	• Must have at least five questions • Must have at least five answers • Should use a system with lights • Should be no larger than a poster board • Holiday lights can be used • $1 contract signed	• Must be written neatly or typed on a piece of paper or an index card • Must have a list of ingredients with measurement for each • Must have numbered steps that explain how to make the recipe
Scrapbook	**Sculpture**	**Song/Rap**
• Cover of scrapbook must have a meaningful title and student's name • Must have at least five themed pages • Each page will have at least one meaningful picture • All photos must have captions	• Must be no larger than 24" tall • Must use recycled materials • Must be created from the number of items given in the task • If appropriate, $1 contract must be submitted with sculpture • Creator's name should be permanently written on the base or bottom	• Words must make sense • Can be presented to an audience or taped • Written words must be turned in before performance or with taped song • Should be at least 2 minutes in length

Figure 3.2. Continued.

Speech	Story	Survey
• Must be at least 2 minutes in length • Should not be read from written paper • Note cards can be used • Written speech must be turned in before speech is presented • Voice must be clear, loud, and easy to understand	• Must have all of the elements of a well-written story (setting, characters, conflict, rising action, and resolution) • Must be appropriate length to allow for story elements • Neatly written or typed	• Must have at least five questions related to the topic • Must include at least one adult respondent who is not your teacher • The respondent must sign the survey • Information gathered and conclusions drawn from the survey should be written or presented graphically

Three-Dimensional Timeline	Three Facts and a Fib	Trading Cards
• Must be no bigger than standard-size poster board • Must be divided into equal time units • Must contain at least 10 important dates and have at least 2 sentences explaining why each date is important • Must have a meaningful object securely attached beside each date to represent that date • Must be able to explain how each object represents each date	• Can be written, typed, or created using PowerPoint • Must include exactly four statements: three true statements and one false statement • False statement should not obvious • Brief paragraph should be included that explains why the fib is false	• Include at least 10 cards • Each card must be at least 3" by 5" • Each should have a colored picture • Includes at least three facts on the subject of the card • Cards must have information on both sides • All cards must be submitted in a carrying bag

Trophy	Venn Diagram	Video
• Must be at least 6" tall • Must have a base with the name of the person getting the trophy and the name of the award written neatly or typed on it • Top of trophy must be appropriate and represent the award • Name should be written on the bottom of the award • Must be an originally designed trophy (avoid reusing a trophy from home)	• Must be at least 8.5" by 11" • Shapes should be thematic and neatly drawn • Must have a title for entire diagram and a title for each section • Must have at least six items in each section of the diagram • Name written on the back	• Use VHS, DVD, or Flash format • Turn in a written plan with project • Students will need to arrange their own way to record the video or allow teacher at least 3 days notice to set up recording • Covers important information about the project • Name written on the video label

Figure 3.2. Continued.

WebQuest	Windowpane	Worksheet
• Must quest through at least three high-quality websites • Websites should be linked in the document • Can be submitted in a Word or PowerPoint document • Includes at least three questions for each website • Must address the topic	• Must be at least 8.5" by 11" unlined paper • Must include at least six squares • Each square must include both a picture and words that should be neatly written or typed • All pictures should be both creative and meaningful • Name should be written on the bottom right-hand corner of the front of the windowpane	• Must be 8.5" by 11" • Neatly written or typed • Must cover the specific topic or question in detail • Must have at least one graphic • An answer key will be turned in with the worksheet
You Be the Person Presentation • Take on the role of the person • Cover at least five important facts about the life of the person • Must be 3–5 minutes in length • Script must be turned in before information is presented • Should be presented to an audience with the ability to answer questions while in character • Must have props or some form of costume		

Figure 3.2. Continued.

CHAPTER 4

Rubrics

> "[Using menus,] I frequently end up with more papers and products to grade than with a unit taught in the traditional way. Luckily, rubrics speed up the process."
>
> —*Eighth-grade teacher*

The most common reason teachers feel uncomfortable with menus is the need for equal grading. Teachers often feel that it is easier to grade the same type of product made by all of the students than to grade a large number of different products, none of which looks like any other. The great equalizer for hundreds of different products is a generic rubric that can cover all of the important qualities of an excellent product.

All-Purpose Rubric

Figure 4.1 is an example of a rubric that has been classroom tested with the menus included in this book. This rubric can be used with any point value activity presented in a menu, as there are five criteria and the columns represent full points, half points, and no points.

There are different ways that this rubric can be shared with students. Some teachers prefer to provide it when a menu is presented to students. The rubric can be reproduced on the back of the menu along with its guidelines. The rubric can also be given to students to keep in their folders with their product guideline cards so they always know the expectations as they complete projects throughout the school year. Some teachers prefer to keep a master copy for themselves and post an enlarged copy of the rubric on a bulletin board, or provide one copy for parents during open house so that they understand how their children's menu products will be graded.

No matter how the rubric is shared with students, the first time they see this rubric, it should be explained to them in detail, especially the last column, titled "Self." It is very important that students self-evaluate their projects. This column can provide a unique perspective on the project as it is being graded. Note: This rubric was designed to be specific enough that students will understand the criteria the teacher is seeking, but general enough that they can still be as creative as they like while making their products.

Student-Taught Lesson and Oral Presentation Rubrics

Although the all-purpose product rubric can be used for all activities, there are two situations that warrant a special rubric: student-taught lessons and oral presentations. These situations have many fine details that must be considered separately.

Student-taught lessons can cause stress for both students and teachers. Teachers would often like to allow students to teach their fellow classmates, but they are not comfortable with the grading aspect of the assignment. Rarely do students understand all of the components that go into designing an effective lesson. This student-taught lesson rubric (see Figure 4.2) helps focus the student on the important aspects of a well-designed lesson and allows teachers to make the evaluation more subjective.

All-Purpose Rubric

Name: _____

Criteria	Excellent (Full Credit)	Good (Half Credit)	Poor (No Credit)	Self
Content Is the content of the product well chosen?	Content chosen represents the best choice for the product. Information or graphics are well chosen and related to content.	Information or graphics are related to content, but are not the best choice for the product.	Information or graphics presented do not appear to be related to the topic or task.	
Completeness Is everything included in the product?	All information needed is included. Product meets the product criteria and the criteria of the task as stated.	Some important information is missing. Product meets the product criteria and the criteria of the task as stated.	Most important information is missing. The product does not meet the task or does not meet the product criteria.	
Creativity Is the product original?	Presentation of information is from a new perspective. Graphics are original. Product includes elements of fun and interest.	Presentation of information is from a new perspective. Graphics are not original. Product has elements of fun and interest.	There is no evidence of new thoughts or perspectives in the product.	
Correctness Is all of the information included correct?	All information presented in the product is correct and accurate.		Any portion of the information presented in the product is incorrect.	
Communication Is the information in the product well communicated?	All information is neat and easy to read. Product is in appropriate format and shows significant effort. Oral presentations are easy to understand and presented with fluency.	Most of the product is neat and easy to read. Product is in appropriate format and shows significant effort. Oral presentations are easy to understand, with some fluency.	The product is not neat and easy to read or the product is not in the appropriate format. It does not show significant effort. Oral presentation was not fluent or easy to understand.	
			Total Grade:	

Figure 4.1. All-purpose product rubric.

Student-Taught Lesson Rubric

Name: _____

Parts of Lesson	Excellent	Good	Fair	Poor	Self
Prepared and Ready All materials and lesson ready at start of class period, from warm-up to conclusion of lesson.	**10** Everything is ready to present.	**6** Lesson is present, but small amount of scrambling.	**3** Lesson is present, but major scrambling.	**0** No lesson ready or missing major components.	
Understanding Presenter understands the material well. Students understand information presented.	**20** All information is correct and in correct format.	**12** Presenter understands; 25% of students do not.	**4** Presenter understands; 50% of students do not.	**0** Presenter is confused.	
Complete Includes all significant information from section or topic.	**15** Includes all important information.	**10** Includes most important information.	**2** Includes less than 50% of the important information.	**0** Information is not related.	
Practice Includes some way for students to practice or access the information.	**20** Practice present; well chosen.	**10** Practice present; can be applied effectively.	**5** Practice present; not related or best choice.	**0** No practice or students are confused.	
Interest/Fun Most of the class is involved, interested, and participating.	**15** Everyone interested and participating.	**10** 75% actively participating.	**5** Less than 50% actively participating.	**0** Everyone off task.	
Creativity Information presented in an imaginative way.	**20** Wow, creative! I never would have thought of that!	**12** Good ideas!	**5** Some good pieces but general instruction.	**0** No creativity; all lecture, notes, or worksheet.	
				Total Grade:	

Your Topic/Objective:

Comments:

Don't Forget:
All copy requests and material requests must be made at least 24 hours in advance.

Figure 4.2. Student-taught lesson rubric.

Within the social studies curriculum, considerable emphasis is placed on presenting information in a spoken manner. The oral presentation rubrics assist with this goal. Two rubrics are included: one for the evaluation of the speaker by the teacher (see Figure 4.3), and one for feedback from the students (see Figure 4.4). This student feedback rubric is included in order to encourage active participation on the part of student observers. This student feedback should always be given in a positive manner. When my students give oral presentations, they actually seem to value their peers' feedback even more than mine!

When using the oral presentation rubrics, please note that the rubric adds to 100 points. With the exception of the 100-point home run option offered on a baseball menu, no single menu products are worth 100 points. In my classroom, I simply explained to my students that the 100-point total was the percentage of total points possible for the activity. If a speech was worth 30 points, then a score of 100 on the oral presentation rubric would earn them 100% of the 30 points, whereas an 80 on the rubric would result in 24 points out of 30. Usually, simply by using the rubric, the students give presentations of a higher quality, as they are made more aware of the elements of a successful presentation.

Student Presentation Rubric

Criteria	Excellent	Good	Fair	Poor	Self
Content Complete Did the presentation include everything it should?	**30** Presentation included all important information about topic being presented.	**20** Presentation covered most of the important information, but one key idea was missing.	**10** Presentation covered some of the important information, but more than one key idea was missing.	**0** Presentation covered information, but the information was trivial or fluff.	
Content Correct Was the information presented accurate?	**30** All information presented was accurate.	**20** All information presented was correct, with a few unintentional errors that were quickly corrected.		**0** Any information presented was not correct.	
Prop Did the speaker have at least one prop that was directly related to the presentation?	**20** Presenter had a prop and it complemented the presentation.	**12** Presenter had a prop, but it was not the best choice.	**4** Presenter had a prop, but there was no clear reason for it.	**0** Presenter had no prop.	
Content Consistent Did the speaker stay on topic?	**10** Presenter stayed on topic 100% of the time.	**7** Presenter stayed on topic 90%–99% of the time.	**4** Presenter stayed on topic 80%–89% of the time.	**0** It was hard to tell what the topic was.	
Flow Was the speaker familiar and comfortable with the material so that it flowed well?	**10** Presentation flowed well. Speaker did not stumble over words.	**7** Presenter had some flow problems, but they did not distract from information.	**4** Some flow problems interrupted the presentation, and presenter seemed flustered.	**0** Constant flow problems occurred, and information was not presented so that it could be understood.	
				Total Grade:	

Figure 4.3. Oral presentation rubric.

© Prufrock Press Inc. • *Differentiating Instruction With Menus for the Inclusive Classroom: Social Studies* • *Grades 6–8*

Topic: _____ **Student's Name:** _____

On a scale of 1–10, rate the following areas:

Content (How in depth was the information? How well did the speaker know the information? Was the information correct? Could the speaker answer questions?)		Give one short reason why you gave this number.
Flow (Did the presentation flow smoothly? Did the speaker appear confident and ready to speak?)		Give one short reason why you gave this number.
Prop (Did the speaker explain his or her prop? Did this choice seem logical? Was it the best choice?)		Give one short reason why you gave this number.

Comments: Below, write two things that you think the presenter did well:

1.

2.

- -

Topic: _____ **Student's Name:** _____

On a scale of 1–10, rate the following areas:

Content (How in depth was the information? How well did the speaker know the information? Was the information correct? Could the speaker answer questions?)		Give one short reason why you gave this number.
Flow (Did the presentation flow smoothly? Did the speaker appear confident and ready to speak?)		Give one short reason why you gave this number.
Prop (Did the speaker explain his or her prop? Did this choice seem logical? Was it the best choice?)		Give one short reason why you gave this number.

Comments: Below, write two things that you think the presenter did well:

1.

2.

Figure 4.4. Student feedback rubric.

The Menus

How to Use the Menu Pages

Each menu in this section has:
- an introduction page for the teacher;
- a lower level content menu, indicated by a triangle (▲) in the upper right-hand corner;
- an on-level content menu, indicated by a circle (●) in the upper right-hand corner;
- any specific guidelines for the menu; and
- activities mentioned in the menu.

Introduction Pages

The introduction pages are meant to provide an overview of each menu. They are divided into five areas:
1. *Objectives Covered Through These Menus and These Activities.* This area will list all of the objectives that the menus can address. Menus are arranged in such a way that if students complete the guidelines set forth in the instructions for the menus, all of these objectives will be covered.

2. *Materials Needed by Students for Completion.* For each menu, it is expected that the teacher will provide, or students will have access to, the following materials:
   - lined paper;
   - glue;
   - crayons, colored pencils, or markers; and
   - blank 8.5" x 11" white paper.

   The introduction page also includes a list of additional materials that may be needed by students as they complete either menu. Any materials listed that are used in only one of the two menus are designated with the menu's corresponding code (either triangle or circle). Students do have the choice about the menu items they can complete, so it is possible that the teacher will not need all of these materials for every student.

3. *Special Notes on the Use of These Menus.* This section will give any special tips on managing student products as well as any specific modification suggestions. This section will also share any tips to consider for a specific activity.

4. *Time Frame.* Most menus are best used in at least a 1-week time frame. Some are better suited to more than 2 weeks. This section will give an overview about the best time frame for completing the entire menu, as well as options for shorter time periods. If teachers do not have time to devote to an entire menu, they can certainly choose the 1–2-day option for any menu topic students are currently studying.

5. *Suggested Forms.* This is a list of the rubrics, templates, and reproducibles that should be available for students as the menus are introduced. If a menu has a free-choice option, the appropriate proposal form also will be listed here.

CHAPTER 5

Geography

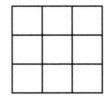

Current Events

Meal Menu ▲ and Tic-Tac-Toe Menu ●

Objective Covered Through These Menus and These Activities

- Students will identify examples of relevant local and international current events.

Materials Needed by Students for Completion

- Poster board or large white paper
- Rulers (for comic strips) ▲
- Materials for bulletin board displays ▲
- World map
- Materials for dioramas (e.g., shoe boxes, cards)
- Internet access (for WebQuests)
- Materials for class games

Special Notes on the Use of These Menus

This topic has two different menu formats: Meal menu and Tic-Tac-Toe menu. The Meal menu is specifically selected for its meal-oriented, Bloom's-based options, as it is easily broken into manageable bits. The menu can be cut into strips, each strip featuring its own meal, to be given to students. This way, once students have chosen and submitted the breakfast product for grading, they can move on to the lunch strip, and lastly, they can complete the dinner and dessert strips. Because this type of menu is designed to become more advanced as students move through the meals, teachers may choose to provide their students who have special needs with just the meals and save the dessert for enrichment.

These menus give students the opportunity to create a class game. The length of the game is not stated in the product guidelines, so the teacher can determine what works best. It may be a good idea to have students start with shorter games and work up to longer games with a review focus.

The triangle menu allows students to create a bulletin board display. Some classrooms may only have one bulletin board, so the teacher can divide the board into sections, or additional classroom wall or hall space can be sectioned off for the creation of these displays. Students can plan their displays based on the amount of space they are assigned.

Time Frame

- 2–3 weeks—Students are given the menus as the unit is started. As the teacher presents lessons throughout the week, he or she should refer back to the menu options associated with that content. The teacher will go over all of the options for that content and have students place check marks in the boxes that represent the activities they are most interested in completing. If students are using the Tic-Tac-Toe menu form, activities chosen and completed should make a column or row. If students are using the Meal menu form, students will complete one product from each meal, with dessert being an optional enrichment product. When students complete these patterns, they will have completed one activity from each content area, learning style, or level of Bloom's Revised taxonomy.
- 1 week—At the start of the unit, the teacher chooses the three activities he or she feels are most valuable for students. Stations can be set up in the classroom. These three activities are available for student choice throughout the week as regular instruction takes place.
- 1–2 days—The teacher chooses an activity from the menu to use with the entire class.

Suggested Forms

- All-purpose rubric
- Oral presentation rubric
- Student feedback rubric
- Free-choice proposal form

Current Events

Directions: Choose one activity each for breakfast, lunch, and dinner. Dessert is an activity you can choose to do after you have finished your other meals. All products must be completed by: _____.

Breakfast

❐ Create a comic strip that shares information about a current event and its impact on your life.

❐ Choose a current event that has a direct impact on you and your classmates. Create Three Facts and a Fib about the current event and its impact on your life.

❐ Create a bulletin board display that shares information about a current event that you believe will have a significant impact on your life 20 years from now.

Lunch

❐ Research various local current events that are impacting your community. In order to obtain the opinions of others, create a questionnaire and ask people about the issue and its impact on their lives. Present your information to your classmates.

❐ Choose a local current event and write a letter or blog to the editor of your local paper about the impact this event is having on the community.

❐ Choose a local current event that is significantly impacting your community. Create a diorama that shows the situation and its impact on your community.

Dinner

❐ Create a class game that quizzes your classmates on various current events occurring around the world and the impact they are having on the United States.

❐ Locate at least five current events that are taking place all over the world. Using a world map, show the locations of the events on the map and write a sentence that explains how each event is impacting the United States.

❐ Free choice—Submit a free-choice proposal about a current event and its impact on the United States to your teacher for approval.

Dessert

❐ Create a WebQuest that takes users through at least one current world event. This WebQuest should focus on the different viewpoints of the event and its impact on the United States.

❐ Choose a local current event and interview one of the people involved in the event. Focus on the impact this event is having on the community.

Name:_____ Date:_____

Current Events

Directions: Check the boxes you plan to complete. They should form a tic-tac-toe across or down. All products are due by: _____.

☐ *Draw It*	☐ *Map It*	☐ *Write It*
Create a cartoon that shares information about a current event and its impact on your life.	Choose at least eight current events that are taking place all over the world. Using a world map, pinpoint the locations of the events on the map and provide a short statement that explains how each event is impacting the United States.	Choose a local current event and write a letter to the editor of your local paper about the impact this event is having on the community.
☐ *Build It*	☐ **Free Choice: Current Events in Your Life** (Fill out your proposal form before beginning the free choice!)	☐ *Play It*
Choose a local current event that is significantly impacting your community. Create a diorama that shows the situation and its impact on your community.		Create a class game that quizzes your classmates on various current events occurring around the world and the impact they are having on the United States.
☐ *Web It*	☐ *Survey It*	☐ *Tell It*
Create a WebQuest that takes questors through at least one current world event. This WebQuest should focus on the different viewpoints pertaining to the event and its impact on the United States.	Research various local current events that are impacting your community. Create a survey and ask people about the issue, their opinions about it, and its impact on their lives. Present your information to your classmates.	Choose a current event that has a direct impact on you and your classmates. Create Three Facts and a Fib about the current event and its impact on your life.

Using Maps

20-50-80 Menus

Objectives Covered Through These Menus and These Activities
- Students will create maps that have legends and appropriate scale.
- Students will compare different projection maps.

Materials Needed by Students for Completion
- Poster board or large white paper
- Microsoft PowerPoint or other slideshow software ●
- Materials for board games (e.g., file folders, colored cards) ▲
- Materials for models
- Materials for bulletin board displays ●
- Local, city, and state maps
- Materials for class games ●

Special Notes on the Use of These Menus
The circle menu allows students to create a bulletin board display. Some classrooms may only have one bulletin board, so the teacher can divide the board into sections, or additional classroom wall or hall space can be sectioned off for the creation of these displays. Students can plan their displays based on the amount of space they are assigned.

The circle menu also allows students to create a class game. The length of the game is not stated in the product guidelines, so the teacher can determine what works best. It may be best to have students start with shorter games and work up to longer games with a review focus.

Time Frame
- 1–2 weeks—Students are given the menus as the unit starts, and the teacher discusses all of the product options. As the different options are discussed, students will choose products that add to a total of 100 points. As the lessons progress, the teacher and students refer back to the menu options associated with the content being taught.
- 1–2 days—The teacher chooses an activity or product from the menu to use with the entire class.

Suggested Forms
- All-purpose rubric
- Point-based free-choice proposal form

Using Maps

Directions: Choose at least two activities from the menu below. The activities must total at least 100 points. Place a check mark next to each box to show which activities you will complete. All activities must be completed by: _____.

---

20 Points

❏ Design a flipbook that shows examples of the different types of maps, as well as the symbols used on each.

❏ Create a how-to brochure that shows how to determine the latitude and longitude of a location using a map.

---

50 Points

❏ Make a Venn diagram to compare and contrast a Mercator map with another projection map of your choice.

❏ Choose three different maps: a local map, a city or state map, and a country map. Create a board game that allows participants to practice their skills with scale, legends, and pinpointing certain locations.

❏ Design a poster for the different types of maps that explains how to determine appropriate scale and how to develop legends.

❏ Free choice—Prepare a proposal form and submit your idea for approval.

---

80 Points

❏ Using your imagination, make a model of an imaginary island. Include and name at least three different types of landforms. Once you have completed your island, create its map with a legend and scale.

❏ Write and present an imaginative children's book about a map that is afraid of being replaced by an electronic map.

Using Maps

Directions: Choose at least two activities from the menu below. The activities must total at least 100 points. Place a check mark next to each box to show which activities you will complete. All activities must be completed by: _____.

---

20 Points

❑ Design a PowerPoint presentation that shows examples of the different types of maps, as well as the symbols and scales used on each.

❑ Create a how-to brochure that shows how to determine the latitude and longitude of a location using a map.

---

50 Points

❑ Create a Venn diagram to compare and contrast a Mercator map with another projection map of your choice.

❑ Choose three different maps: a local map, a city or state map, and a country map. Create a class game that allows participants to practice their skills with scale, legends, and pinpointing certain locations.

❑ Design a bulletin board display for the different types of maps that explains how to determine appropriate scale and how to develop legends.

❑ Free choice—Prepare a proposal form and submit your idea for approval.

---

80 Points

❑ Using your imagination, make a model of an imaginary island. Include and name at least three different types of landforms. Once you have completed your island, create its map with a legend and scale.

❑ Is using and understanding a map becoming less important? Write and present a speech from the point of view of a paper map discussing its importance to the world.

My Country in Depth

Game Show Menus

Objectives Covered Through These Menus and These Activities

- Students will identify and share various cultural aspects about their country, including art, music, and literature.
- Students will share significant events in the history of their country.
- Students will identify areas of their country that would be most interesting for others to visit.
- Students will identify and share political and religious traditions of their country.

Materials Needed by Students for Completion

- Poster board or large white paper
- Materials for creating a map
- Microsoft PowerPoint or other slideshow software
- Materials for three-dimensional timelines
- Materials for museum exhibits (e.g., boxes, cards)
- Scrapbooking materials
- Blank index cards (for trading cards)
- Graph paper or Internet access (for crossword puzzles)
- DVD or VHS recorder (for commercials and news reports)
- Magazine (for collages) ▲

Special Notes on the Use of These Menus

These menus give students the opportunity to create a news report or commercial. Although students enjoy producing their own videos, there are often difficulties obtaining the equipment and scheduling the use of the video recorder. The menus can be modified by allowing students to act out their new reports or commercials (like a play), or if students have the technology, they may wish to produce a webcam or Flash version of their news reports or commercials.

Time Frame

- 2–3 weeks—Students are given the menus as the unit is started, and the guidelines and point expectations are discussed. As lessons are taught throughout the unit, students and the teacher can refer back to the options associated with the topic. The teacher will go over all of the options for the topic being covered and will have students place check marks in the boxes next to the activities they are most interested in completing. As teaching continues throughout the 2–3 weeks, activities are discussed, chosen, and submitted for grading.

- 1 week—At the beginning of the unit, the teacher chooses an activity from each area that he or she feels would be most valuable for students. Stations can be set up in the classroom. These activities are available for student choice throughout the week as regular instruction takes place.
- 1–2 days—The teacher chooses an activity from an objective to use with the entire class during lesson time.

Suggested Forms

- All-purpose rubric
- Student-taught lesson rubric
- Oral presentation rubric
- Student feedback rubric
- Point-based free-choice proposal form

Name:_____ Date:_____

Guidelines for the My Country in Depth Game Show Menu

- You must choose at least one activity from each topic area.
- You may not do more than two activities in any one topic area for credit. (You are, of course, welcome to do more than two for your own investigation.)
- Grading will be ongoing, so turn in products as you complete them.
- All free-choice proposals must be turned in and approved *prior* to working on that free-choice product.
- You must earn 120 points for a 100%. You may earn extra credit up to _____ points.
- You must show your teacher your plan for completion by: _____.

My Country in Depth

Geography	History	Politics	Religion and Traditions	Music, Art, Literature, and Architecture	Points of Interest	Points for Each Level
☐ Draw a map of your country focusing on its geography and features. (15 pts.)	☐ Design a three-dimensional timeline that shows the major events in your country's history. (15 pts.)	☐ Create a set of trading cards for the political parties and government officials in your country. (15 pts.)	☐ Creat a mind map for the religions and traditions found in your country. (15 pts.)	☐ Create a flipbook with information and examples of the music, art, literature, and architecture of your country. (10 pts.)	☐ Create a crossword puzzle with descriptions of at least 10 locations in your country that students your age would enjoy visiting. (15 pts.)	10–15 points
☐ Create a PowerPoint presentation that shows and explains the geographical regions of your country and their importance. (25 pts.)	☐ Pretend you have lived through all of the major events in your country's history. Create a scrapbook that details these major events from your point of view. (25 pts.)	☐ Choose a current governmental event in your country. Make a poster to tell about the event and share your opinion about it. (20 pts.)	☐ Design an appropriate greeting card for one of the religious traditions found in your country. (25 pts.)	☐ Create a collage that shares why your country's art, music, and architecture are special. (25 pts.)	☐ Create a PowerPoint presentation in which you present information on the various points of interest in your country. (25 pts.)	20–25 points
☐ Design a class lesson on the geography of your country. Compare and contrast its different regions. (30 pts.)	☐ Design a museum exhibit for your country's national museum that shares an important but not well-known historical event. (30 pts.)	☐ Choose the person you feel has had the greatest impact on politics in your country. Develop a You Be the Person presentation to share his or her contributions to the country. (30 pts.)	☐ Write a children's book about a child from your country participating in one of his or her religious traditions. (30 pts.)	☐ Research the music and songs that are currently popular in your country. Write and perform a song or rap that matches a popular style. (30 pts.)	☐ Design a commercial that promotes your country and its points of interest. (30 pts.)	30 points
Free Choice (prior approval) (25–50 pts.)	**Free Choice** (prior approval) (25–50 pts.)	**Free Choice** (prior approval) (25–50 pts.)	**Free Choice** (prior approval) (25–50 pts.)	**Free Choice** (prior approval) (25–50 pts.)	**Free Choice** (prior approval) (25–50 pts.)	25–50 points
Total:	Total:	Total:	Total:	Total:	Total:	Total Grade:

Name:_____ Date:_____

My Country in Depth

Geography	History	Politics	Religion and Traditions	Music, Art, Literature, and Architecture	Points of Interest	Points for Each Level
☐ Draw a map of your country focusing on its geography and features. (10 pts.)	☐ Design a three-dimensional timeline that shows the major events in your country's history. (15 pts.)	☐ Create a set of trading cards for the political parties and responsibilities of the government officials in your country. (15 pts.)	☐ Write Three Facts and a Fib for the religions and traditions found in your country. (15 pts.)	☐ Create a flipbook with information about and examples of the music, art, literature, and architecture of your country. (10 pts.)	☐ Create a crossword puzzle with descriptions of at least 15 locations students your age would enjoy visiting in your country. (15 pts.)	**10–15 points**
☐ Create a PowerPoint presentation that shows and explains the geographical regions of your country and their importance. (20 pts.)	☐ Design a museum exhibit for your country's national museum that shares an important but not well-known historical event. (25 pts.)	☐ Create a political scrapbook that shares how your country's government and different officials are structured. (25 pts.)	☐ Design an appropriate greeting card for one of the religious traditions found in your country. (25 pts.)	☐ Research the music and songs that are currently popular in your country. Write and perform a song or rap that matches a popular style. (25 pts.)	☐ Design a commercial that promotes your country and its points of interest. (20 pts.)	**20–25 points**
☐ Design a class lesson on the geography of your country. Compare and contrast its different regions. (30 pts.)	☐ Write and perform a play to reenact the historical event that, in your opinion, has had the greatest impact on your country. (30 pts.)	☐ Choose the person you feel has had the greatest impact on politics in your country. Develop a You Be the Person presentation to share his or her contributions. (30 pts.)	☐ Write a story about a teenager from your country participating in one of his or her religious traditions. (30 pts.)	☐ Artists often express their thoughts and feelings by painting murals on the sides of buildings. Create your own mural on paper that reflects your thoughts about life in your country. (30 pts.)	☐ Your country's government is considering renovating its most famous tourist attraction. Create a news report on the proposed renovations and the public's response. (30 pts.)	**30 points**
Free Choice (prior approval) (25–50 pts.)	**Free Choice** (prior approval) (25–50 pts.)	**Free Choice** (prior approval) (25–50 pts.)	**Free Choice** (prior approval) (25–50 pts.)	**Free Choice** (prior approval) (25–50 pts.)	**Free Choice** (prior approval) (25–50 pts.)	**25–50 points**
Total:	Total:	Total:	Total:	Total:	Total:	Total Grade:

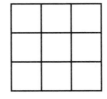

United States Geography

Meal Menu ▲ and Tic-Tac-Toe Menu ●

Objectives Covered Through These Menus and These Activities

- Students will recognize different landforms and natural resources found in the United States.
- Students will understand that there are different climates found in the United States.

Materials Needed by Students for Completion

- Poster board or large white paper
- Materials for models
- Map of the United States
- Materials for three-dimensional timelines
- Microsoft PowerPoint or other slideshow software ▲
- Materials for board games (e.g. folders, colored cards)
- DVD or VHS recorder (for commercials) ●
- Materials for bulletin board displays
- Product cube template

Special Notes on the Use of These Menus

This topic has two different menu formats: Meal menu and Tic-Tac-Toe menu. The Meal menu is specifically selected for its meal-oriented, Bloom's-based options, as it is easily broken into manageable bits. The menu can be cut into strips, each strip featuring its own meal, to be given to students. This way, once students have chosen and submitted the breakfast product for grading, they can move on to the lunch strip, and lastly, they can complete the dinner and dessert strips. Because this type of menu is designed to become more advanced as students move through the meals, teachers may choose to provide their students who have special needs with just the meals and save the dessert for enrichment.

These menus allow students to create a bulletin board display. Some classrooms may only have one bulletin board, so the teacher can divide the board into sections, or additional classroom wall or hall space can be sectioned off for the creation of these displays. Students can plan their displays based on the amount of space they are assigned. These menus also give students the opportunity to create a commercial. Although students enjoy producing their own videos, there are often difficulties obtaining the equipment and scheduling the use of the video recorder. The menus can be modified by allowing students to act out their commercials (like a play), or if students have the technology, they may wish to produce a webcam or Flash version of their commercials.

Time Frame

- 2–3 weeks—Students are given the menus as the unit is started. As the teacher presents lessons throughout the week, he or she should refer back to the menu options associated with that content. The teacher will go over all of the options for that content and have students place check marks in the boxes that represent the activities they are most interested in completing. If students are using the Tic-Tac-Toe menu form, activities chosen and completed should make a column or row. If students are using the Meal menu form, students will complete one product from each meal, with dessert being an optional enrichment product. When students complete these patterns, they will have completed one activity from each content area, learning style, or level of Bloom's Revised taxonomy.
- 1 week—At the start of the unit, the teacher chooses the three activities he or she feels are most valuable for students. Stations can be set up in the classroom. These three activities are available for student choice throughout the week as regular instruction takes place.
- 1–2 days—The teacher chooses an activity from the menu to use with the entire class.

Suggested Forms

- All-purpose rubric
- Free-choice proposal form
- Oral presentation rubric
- Student feedback rubric

United States Geography

Directions: Choose one activity each for breakfast, lunch, and dinner. Dessert is an activity you can choose to do after you have finished your other meals. All products must be completed by: _____.

Breakfast

❑ Create a model of three different landforms that are unique to the United States.

❑ Using a map of the United States, locate and mark at least three different landforms. Write a short paragraph about each one.

❑ Create a landform cube for a common landform found in your state. Follow the pattern on the cube to analyze your landform.

Lunch

❑ Create a game show that asks contestants to recognize different areas of the United States based on clues about the areas' climates.

❑ If you could live anywhere in the United States based on its climate, where would you choose? Create a brochure to advertise your choice, including information about why this climate is the best.

❑ Free choice—Submit a free-choice proposal about our country's different climates to your teacher for approval.

Dinner

❑ Design a bulletin board display that shows the various natural resources found in your home state, as well as the country as a whole. Include at least one graph in your display.

❑ Research the United States' natural resources, especially those that have diminished over time. Create a three-dimensional timeline that shows the use of your state's and the United States' resources.

❑ Create a natural resources board game. Players should use natural resource maps in order to progress through the game.

Dessert

❑ There are various reasons why people choose to move to different areas of the U.S., including climate. Write and perform a play about a family who has decided to move based on climate. Be creative and have fun with the family's decision!

❑ Design a PowerPoint presentation that compares the distribution of natural resources in your state with other states across the country.

Name:_____ Date:_____ ●

United States Geography

Directions: Check the boxes you plan to complete. They should form a tic-tac-toe across or down. All products are due by: _____.

☐ *Our Landforms*	☐ *Our Climate*	☐ *Our Natural Resources*
Create a model of three different landforms that are unique to the United States.	There are various reasons why people choose to move to different areas of the U.S., including climate. Write and perform a play about a family who has decided to move based on climate. Be creative and have fun with the family's decision!	Create a natural resources board game. Players should use natural resource maps in order to progress through the game.
☐ *Our Natural Resources*	☐ **Free Choice: United States Landforms** (Fill out your proposal form before beginning the free choice!)	☐ *Our Climate*
Research the United States' natural resources, especially those that have diminished over time. Create a three-dimensional timeline that shows the progression and use of your state's and the United States' resources.		If you could live anywhere in the United States based on its climate, where would you choose? Create a commercial for your choice sharing why the climate is the best.
☐ *Our Climate*	☐ *Our Natural Resources*	☐ *Our Landforms*
Create a game show that has contestants recognize different areas of the United States based on clues about the climate in that area.	Design a bulletin board display that shows the various natural resources found in your home state, as well as the country as a whole. Include at least two graphs in your display.	Create a landform cube for a common landform found in your state. Follow the pattern on the cube to analyze your landform in depth.

Landform Cube

Complete the cube for a common landform in your country. Respond to the prompts on each side to analyze your landform in depth. Use this pattern or create your own cube.

Provide measurements for one of your landforms.

Explain how your landform is created.

Draw a picture of your landform.

Explain why this landform is so common in your state.

How does this landform impact the ecosystem?

List at least eight locations in your state where this landform can be found.

CHAPTER 6

Government

Economics

20-50-80 Menus

Objectives Covered Through These Menus and These Activities
- Students will understand the concepts of supply and demand.
- Students will compare and contrast capitalism and socialism.

Materials Needed by Students for Completion
- Poster board or large white paper
- Magazines (for collages)
- DVD or VHS recorder (for news reports) ●
- Materials for museum exhibits (e.g., boxes, cards) ▲
- Bags or socks (for puppets) ▲
- Materials for class games ●

Special Notes on the Use of These Menus
The circle menu gives students the opportunity to create a class game. The length of the game is not stated in the product guidelines, so the teacher can determine what works best. It may be a good idea to have students start with shorter games and work up to longer games with a review focus.

The circle menu also gives students the opportunity to create a news report. Although students enjoy producing their own videos, there are often difficulties obtaining the equipment and scheduling the use of the video recorder. The menus can be modified by allowing students to act out their news reports (like a play), or if students have the technology, they may wish to produce a webcam or Flash version of their news reports.

Time Frame
- 1–2 weeks—Students are given the menus as the unit is started, and the teacher discusses all of the product options on the menus. As the different options are discussed, students will choose products that add to a total of 100 points. As the lessons progress, the teacher and students refer back to the menu options associated with the content being taught.

- 1–2 days—The teacher chooses an activity or product from the menu to use with the entire class.

Suggested Forms

- All-purpose rubric
- Point-based free-choice proposal form
- Oral presentation rubric
- Student feedback rubric

Economics

Directions: Choose at least two activities from the menu below. The activities must total at least 100 points. Place a check mark next to each box to show which activities you will complete. All activities must be completed by: _____.

20 Points

❑ Create a Venn diagram to compare capitalism and socialism. Include at least four real-world examples of each.

❑ Create a poster that would help your classmates understand supply and demand.

50 Points

❑ Design a song or rap that teaches the advantages and disadvantages of both socialism and capitalism.

❑ Look through magazines and locate advertisements for products that have been impacted significantly by supply and demand. Using a large piece of paper, make a collage out of these advertisements and include a brief statement on the back that explains how each item was impacted.

❑ Design a puppet to discuss socialism's economic benefits versus those of capitalism.

❑ Free choice—Prepare a proposal form and submit your idea for approval.

80 Points

❑ You have been invited to create a museum exhibit for the United States Money Museum. They are interested in an exhibit on the history of socialism and its benefits. Create the exhibit.

❑ Write a children's book about a character who creates an invention that is in high demand and the funny things that happen as the character tries to keep up the supply.

Economics

Directions: Choose at least two activities from the menu below. The activities must total at least 100 points. Place a check mark next to each box to show which activities you will complete. All activities must be completed by: _____.

---

20 Points

❒ Create a Venn diagram to compare capitalism and socialism. Include at least four real-world examples of each.

❒ Create a worksheet that would help your classmates distinguish capitalism from socialism.

---

50 Points

❒ Design a song or rap that teaches the advantages and disadvantages of both socialism and capitalism.

❒ Look through magazines and locate advertisements for products that have been impacted significantly by supply and demand. Using poster board, make a collage out of these advertisements and include a brief statement on the back that explains how each item was impacted.

❒ Create a class game that tests your classmates' knowledge of socialism and capitalism and how each philosophy can affect a country.

❒ Free choice—Prepare a proposal form and submit your idea for approval.

---

80 Points

❒ Any age group can affect supply and demand. Determine two products on which you and your classmates have had a direct impact. Create a news report that interviews a classmate about your peers' impact on the process of supply and demand.

❒ Write a story about a teenager who moves from a country with a socialist economy to one with a capitalist society and how this impacts his or her possible future occupations.

Citizenship

List Menus

Objectives Covered Through These Menus and These Activities
- Students will identify the qualities and responsibilities of good citizens.
- Students will identify people they consider to be good citizens and defend their choices.

Materials Needed by Students for Completion
- Poster board or large white paper
- Magazines (for collages)
- Microsoft PowerPoint or other slideshow software
- Blank index cards (for trading cards)
- Graph paper or Internet access (for crossword puzzles)
- Materials for trophies
- Materials for three-dimensional timelines
- DVD or VHS recorder (for commercials)
- Product cube template
- Materials for class games

Special Notes on the Use of These Menus
These menus give students the opportunity to create a class game. The length of the game is not stated in the product guidelines, so the teacher can determine what works best. It may be a good idea to have students start with shorter games and work up to longer games with a review focus.

These menus also give students the opportunity to create a commercial. Although students enjoy producing their own videos, there are often difficulties obtaining the equipment and scheduling the use of the video recorder. The menus can be modified by allowing students to act out their commercials (like a play), or if students have the technology, they may wish to produce a webcam or Flash version of their commercials.

Time Frame
- 1–2 weeks—Students are given the menus as the unit is started, and guidelines and point expectations are discussed. Students will usually

need to earn 100 points for 100%, although there is an opportunity for extra credit if the teacher would like to use another target number. Because these menus cover one topic in depth, the teacher will go over all of the options on the menus and have students place check marks in the boxes next to the activities they are most interested in completing. Teachers will need to set aside a few moments with each student to sign the agreement at the bottom of the page. As instruction continues, activities are completed by students and submitted for grading.

- 1–2 days—The teacher chooses an activity or product from an objective to use with the entire class during lesson time.

Suggested Forms

- All-purpose rubric
- Point-based free-choice proposal form
- Oral presentation rubric
- Student feedback rubric

Citizenship: Side 1

Guidelines:
1. You may complete as many of the activities listed as you can within the time period.
2. You may choose any combination of activities.
3. Your goal is 100 points. You may earn up to _____ points extra credit.
4. You may be as creative as you like within the guidelines listed below.
5. You must show your plan to your teacher by _____.
6. Activities may be turned in at any time during the working time period. They will be graded and recorded on this sheet as you continue to work, so keep it safe!

Plan to Do	Activity to Complete (Side 1: 10–25 points)	Point Value	Date Completed	Points Earned
	Complete another student's crossword puzzle.	10		
	Create a poster of a good citizen. Show at least eight characteristics a good citizen would possess.	15		
	Create a set of trading cards for famous good citizens.	15		
	Create Three Facts and a Fib about the responsibilities of being a good citizen.	20		
	Create a good citizen cube. Place situations on each side where a person is being either a good citizen or a bad citizen. Be sure the bad citizen isn't too obvious! Provide an answer key for your cube explaining why each is good or bad.	20		
	Design a book cover for a new book called *How to Be a Good Citizen and Still Be Popular!*	20		
	Choose someone that everyone in your class knows. Create a "Good Citizen" trophy for this person and write a short paragraph.	25		
	Create a crossword puzzle for good citizens and their traits.	25		
	Create a three-dimensional timeline of good citizens in the past 400 years featuring at least six people. Include a brief statement for each about why he or she was selected.	25		
	Design a greeting card that could be given to someone who has demonstrated good citizenship.	25		
	Make a collage of good citizens. Include a statement that explains why you selected each person for your collage.	25		
	Using Microsoft PowerPoint or other slideshow software, create a good citizen quiz for your classmates that uses realistic situations.	25		
	Total number of points you are planning to earn from Side 1.	**Total points earned from Side 1:**		

Name:_____ Date:_____ ▲

Citizenship: Side 2

Plan to Do	Activity to Complete (Side 2: 30 points and up)	Point Value	Date Completed	Points Earned
	Produce a class game that has your classmates deciding which situations demonstrate good citizenship. Don't make it too obvious!	30		
	Write and perform a play that features good citizens, as well as citizens who do not exhibit those same positive characteristics.	30		
	Choose a musician who has the qualities of a good citizen in your opinion. Prepare a You Be the Person presentation in which you come to class as that person and discuss the characteristics of a good citizen.	35		
	Create a commercial promoting good citizenship that would be appropriate and interesting to others your age.	35		
	Survey your classmates to discover which characteristics of a good citizen they feel are most valuable. Share your findings on a poster.	35		
	Write a story about a teenager who takes on the responsibilities of a good citizen even though it may not be an easy choice for him or her.	35		
	Free choice: must be outlined on a proposal form and approved before beginning work.	10–40 points		
	Total number of points you are planning to earn from Side 1.		**Total points earned from Side 1:**	
	Total number of points you are planning to earn from Side 2.		**Total points earned from Side 2:**	
			Grand Total (/100)	

I am planning to complete _____ activities that could earn up to a total of _____ points.

Teacher's initials _____ Student's signature _____

Name:_____ Date:_____

Citizenship: Side 1

Guidelines:

1. You may complete as many of the activities listed as you can within the time period.
2. You may choose any combination of activities.
3. Your goal is 100 points. You may earn up to _____ points extra credit.
4. You may be as creative as you like within the guidelines listed below.
5. You must show your plan to your teacher by _____.
6. Activities may be turned in at any time during the working time period. They will be graded and recorded on this sheet as you continue to work, so keep it safe!

Plan to Do	Activity to Complete (Side 1: 10–25 points)	Point Value	Date Completed	Points Earned
	Complete another student's crossword puzzle.	10		
	Create a poster of a good citizen. Show at least 10 characteristics a good citizen would possess.	10		
	Create a good citizen cube. Place situations on each side where a person is being either a good citizen or a bad citizen. Be sure the bad citizen isn't too obvious! Provide an answer key for your cube explaining why each is good or bad.	15		
	Create a set of trading cards for famous good citizens.	15		
	Create Three Facts and a Fib about the responsibilities of being a good citizen.	15		
	Choose someone that everyone in your class knows. Create a "Good Citizen" trophy for this person and write a short paragraph about why he or she should receive the trophy.	20		
	Create a crossword puzzle for good citizens and their traits.	20		
	Design a book cover for a new book called *How to Be a Good Citizen and Still Be Popular!*	20		
	Make a collage of good citizens. Include a statement that explains why you selected each person.	20		
	Using Microsoft PowerPoint or other slideshow software, create a good citizen quiz for your classmates using realistic situations.	20		
	Create a three-dimensional timeline of good citizens in the past 400 years featuring at least 10 people. Include a brief statement for each about why the person was selected for your timeline.	25		
	Design a greeting card that could be given to someone who has demonstrated good citizenship.	25		
	Total number of points you are planning to earn from Side 1.	**Total points earned from Side 1:**		

Name:_____ Date:_____ ●

Citizenship: Side 2

Plan to Do	Activity to Complete (Side 2: 30 points and up)	Point Value	Date Completed	Points Earned
	Choose a musician who has the qualities of a good citizen in your opinion. Prepare a You Be the Person presentation in which you come to class as that person and discuss the characteristics of a good citizen.	30		
	Create a commercial promoting good citizenship that would be appropriate and interesting to others your age.	30		
	Survey your classmates to discover which characteristics of a good citizen they feel are most valuable. Share your findings on a poster.	30		
	Produce a class game that has your classmates deciding which situations demonstrate good citizenship. Don't make it too obvious!	30		
	Write and perform a play that features good citizens, as well as citizens who do not exhibit those same positive characteristics.	30		
	Write a story about a teenager who takes on the responsibilities of a good citizen even though it may not be an easy choice for him or her.	30		
	Free choice: must be outlined on a proposal form and approved before beginning work.	10–40 points		
	Total number of points you are planning to earn from Side 1.	**Total points earned from Side 1:**		
	Total number of points you are planning to earn from Side 2.	**Total points earned from Side 2:**		
		Grand Total (/100)		

I am planning to complete _____ activities that could earn up to a total of _____ points.

Teacher's initials _____ Student's signature _____

Citizenship Cube

Place a situation on each side. Some should be examples of good citizenship, others of bad citizenship (but do not be too obvious!). Provide an answer key for your cube explaining why each situation is good or bad. Use this pattern or create your own cube.

Immigration

20-50-80 Menus

Objectives Covered Through These Menus and These Activities

- Students will share some of the reasons why people have immigrated and continue to immigrate to this country.
- Students will understand the experiences of people who have immigrated to this country.
- Students will understand the experiences of immigrants from an immigrant's perspective.
- Students will identify some of the historical trends that have occurred in patterns of immigration to America.

Materials Needed by Students for Completion

- Poster board or large white paper
- Coat hangers (for mobiles) ▲
- Blank index cards (for mobiles) ▲
- String (for mobiles) ▲
- DVD or VHS recorder (for news reports)
- Access to library or fictional books about immigrants
- Internet access (for research)
- Magazines (for collages) ●
- Microsoft PowerPoint or other slideshow software ●

Special Notes on the Use of These Menus

These menus give students the opportunity to create a news report. Although students enjoy producing their own videos, there are often difficulties obtaining the equipment and scheduling the use of the video recorder. The menus can be modified by allowing students to act out their videos (like a play), or if students have the technology, they may wish to produce a webcam or Flash version of their news reports.

Time Frame

- 1–2 weeks—Students are given the menus as the unit is started, and the teacher discusses all of the product options on the menus. As the different options are discussed, students will choose products that add to a total of 100 points. As the lessons progress, the teacher and

students refer back to the menu options associated with the content being taught.
- 1–2 days—The teacher chooses an activity or product from the menu to use with the entire class.

Suggested Forms

- All-purpose rubric
- Oral presentation rubric
- Student feedback rubric
- Point-based free-choice proposal form

Immigration

Directions: Choose at least two activities from the menu below. The activities must total at least 100 points. Place a check mark next to each box to show which activities you will complete. All activities must be completed by: _____.

---

20 Points

❏ Create a mobile that shows various reasons why immigrants leave their home and come to the United States. Include an historical example with each of your reasons.

❏ Design a map that shows the historical trends of immigration throughout the history of the United States.

---

50 Points

❏ Choose two different groups that immigrated to our country. Create a Venn diagram to compare and contrast their reasons for leaving their homes, their journey, and what they may have hoped to find in our country.

❏ Determine the different reasons people have had throughout history for leaving their home country. Create an advertisement for a company that is willing to help people immigrate to the United States.

❏ You have been assigned to cover what is happening at Ellis Island on a daily basis in 1911. Create a news report for what you observe.

❏ Free choice—Prepare a proposal form and submit your idea for approval.

---

80 Points

❏ A book may be classified as fiction; however, the author may have based the story on real-life experiences or events. Choose a fictional book about a person your age immigrating to the United States. Evaluate the book to distinguish the facts from the fiction contained in the story.

❏ Visit the Ellis Island passenger record website (http://www.ellisisland.org). After entering a name of your choice (try a family name!) and choosing a passenger, record all of the information about that person. Present a You Be the Person presentation about this person, including life before immigrating and hopes for life in the United States.

Immigration

Directions: Choose at least two activities from the menu below. The activities must total at least 100 points. Place a check mark next to each box to show which activities you will complete. All activities must be completed by: _____.

---

20 Points

❏ Create a collage that shows various reasons why immigrants leave their home and come to the United States. Include an historical example with each of your reasons.

❏ Design a map that shows the historical trends of immigration throughout the history of the United States.

---

50 Points

❏ A book may be classified as fiction; however, the author may have based the story on real-life experiences or events. Choose a fictional book about a person your age immigrating to the United States. Evaluate the book to distinguish the facts from the fiction contained in the story.

❏ Determine the different reasons people have had throughout history for leaving their home country. Create a PowerPoint advertisement for a company that is willing to help people immigrate to the United States.

❏ You have been assigned to cover what is happening at Ellis Island on a daily basis in 1911. Create a news report for what you observe.

❏ Free choice—Prepare a proposal form and submit your idea for approval.

---

80 Points

❏ Investigate the different eras during history when there have been large numbers of immigrants coming to the United States. Write a children's book about the immigration of someone your age during one of these historical time periods. Include the reasons that person is leaving his or her home country, describe his or her journey, and share his or her first impressions of our country.

❏ Visit the Ellis Island passenger record website (http://www.ellisisland.org). After entering a name of your choice (try a family name!) and choosing a passenger, record all of the information about that person. Present a You Be the Person presentation about this person, including life before immigrating, the journey, and hopes for life in the United States.

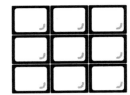

Our Government

Game Show Menus

Objectives Covered Through These Menus and These Activities

- Students will state the principles of government and how they impact their community.
- Students will identify examples of the rights guaranteed through government documents.
- Students will understand how the different levels of government interact with each other.
- Students will have an understanding of how revenue is generated at the different levels of government.
- Students will identify the different political parties and explain their current views.

Materials Needed by Students for Completion

- Poster board or large white paper
- Newspapers
- Coat hangers (for mobiles)
- Blank index cards (for mobiles)
- String (for mobiles)
- Internet access (for WebQuests)
- DVD or VHS recorder (for commercials) ▲
- Materials for bulletin board displays ▲
- Scrapbooking materials

Special Notes on the Use of These Menus

These menus allow students to create a WebQuest. There are multiple versions and templates for WebQuests available on the Internet. Teachers should decide whether to specify a certain format or allow students to create one of their own choosing.

The triangle menu allows students to create a bulletin board display. Some classrooms may only have one bulletin board, so the teacher can divide the board into sections, or additional classroom wall or hall space can be sectioned off for the creation of these displays. Students can plan their displays based on the amount of space they are assigned.

The triangle menu also gives students the opportunity to create a commercial. Although students enjoy producing their own videos, there are often difficulties obtaining the equipment and scheduling the use of the video recorder. The menu can be modified by allowing students to act out their commercials (like a play), or if students have the technology, then they may wish to produce a webcam or Flash version of their commercials.

Time Frame

- 2–3 weeks—Students are given the menus as the unit is started, and the guidelines and point expectations are discussed. As lessons are taught throughout the unit, students and the teacher can refer back to the options associated with the topic. The teacher will go over all of the options for the topic being covered and will have students place check marks in the boxes next to the activities they are most interested in completing. As teaching continues throughout the 2–3 weeks, activities are discussed, chosen, and submitted for grading.
- 1 week—At the beginning of the unit, the teacher chooses an activity from each area that he or she feels would be most valuable for students. Stations can be set up in the classroom. These activities are available for student choice throughout the week as regular instruction takes place.
- 1–2 days—The teacher chooses an activity from an objective to use with the entire class during lesson time.

Suggested Forms

- All-purpose rubric
- Oral presentation rubric
- Student feedback rubric
- Point-based free-choice proposal form

Name:_____ Date:_____

Guidelines for the Our Government Game Show Menu

- You must choose at least one activity from each topic area.
- You may not do more than two activities in any one topic area for credit. (You are, of course, welcome to do more than two for your own investigation.)
- Grading will be ongoing, so turn in products as you complete them.
- All free-choice proposals must be turned in and approved *prior* to working on that free-choice product.
- You must earn 100 points for a 100%. You may earn extra credit up to _____ points.
- You must show your teacher your plan for completion by: _____.

Our Government

Principles of Government	Rights of the People	Structures and Functions of Government	Government Revenue	Political Parties	Points for Each Level
☐ Make a windowpane for the seven principles of government. (10 pts.)	☐ Create Three Facts and a Fib about the U.S. Constitution. (15 pts.)	☐ Make a mobile that shows the structures and functions of the government at municipal, county, and state levels. (15 pts.)	☐ Create a pie graph of the different sources of revenue for your state. Include a pictorial representation for each area of the graph. (15 pts.)	☐ Make a mind map of the different political parties and their viewpoints. (15 pts.)	10–15 points
☐ Create a song or rap to help your classmates learn and remember the seven principles of government and what each means to us. (20 pts.)	☐ Create a scrapbook of newspaper articles that show examples of people's rights. (25 pts.)	☐ Make a survey to find out what people think are the functions of the government. Write a paragraph sharing your information. (25 pts.)	☐ Research how your local government receives its revenue. Make a poster showing a new way it could earn revenue. (20 pts.)	☐ Design a political cartoon that represents the viewpoint of one of the political parties on an issue that is important to you. (25 pts.)	20–25 points
☐ Prepare a speech to share with your classmates that explains what you feel is the most important principle of government. (30 pts.)	☐ Look through a newspaper and find examples of people's rights being protected. Design a bulletin board display to share your findings. (30 pts.)	☐ Create a WebQuest that shows questors how the different levels of government are interrelated. (30 pts.)	☐ Create a radio or television commercial promoting a raise in the state sales tax. (30 pts.)	☐ Research past governors of your state and the political parties they represented. Is there a pattern? In a report, develop a hypothesis for this pattern. (30 pts.)	30 points
Free Choice (prior approval) (25–50 pts.)	Free Choice (prior approval) (25–50 pts.)	Free Choice (prior approval) (25–50 pts.)	Free Choice (prior approval) (25–50 pts.)	Free Choice (prior approval) (25–50 pts.)	25–50 points
Total:	Total:	Total:	Total:	Total:	Total Grade:

Our Government

Name:_____ Date:_____

Principles of Government	Rights of the People	Structures and Functions of Government	Government Revenue	Political Parties	Points for Each Level
☐ Make a windowpane for the seven principles of government. (10 pts.)	☐ Create a thematic Venn diagram to compare and contrast the U.S. Constitution with your state's constitution. (15 pts.)	☐ Make a mobile that shows the structures and functions of the government at municipal, county, and state levels. (10 pts.)	☐ Create a pie graph of the different sources of revenue for your state. Include a pictorial representation for each area of the graph. (15 pts.)	☐ Make a mind map of the different political parties and their viewpoints. (10 pts.)	10–15 points
☐ Find an example of checks and balances that has taken place in the past year in your state. Create a poster that explains the example. (20 pts.)	☐ Create a scrapbook of newspaper articles that shows examples of people's rights. (20 pts.)	☐ Create a song or rap to help your classmates learn and remember the functions of the government at different levels. (20 pts.)	☐ Research how your local government receives its revenue. Make a brochure to share a new way it could earn revenue. (25 pts.)	☐ Design a political cartoon that represents the viewpoint of one of the political parties on an issue that is important to you. (25 pts.)	20–25 points
☐ Prepare a speech to share with your classmates that explains what you feel is the most important principle of government. (30 pts.)	☐ Create a dramatic presentation that shows which right is most important to people your age. (30 pts.)	☐ Create a WebQuest that shows questors how the different levels of government are interrelated. (30 pts.)	☐ Is it possible for a person to live in your state and not ever legally provide the government revenue? Write a newspaper article in which you interview a person who is doing this. (30 pts.)	☐ Research past governors of your state and the political parties they represented. Is there a pattern? In a report, develop a hypothesis for this pattern. (30 pts.)	30 points
Free Choice (prior approval) (25–50 pts.)	Free Choice (prior approval) (25–50 pts.)	Free Choice (prior approval) (25–50 pts.)	Free Choice (prior approval) (25–50 pts.)	Free Choice (prior approval) (25–50 pts.)	25–50 points
Total:	Total:	Total:	Total:	Total:	Total Grade:

Our Country's Presidents

Meal Menu ▲ and Tic-Tac-Toe Menu ●

Objectives Covered Through These Menus and These Activities
- Students will investigate the qualities of an effective president.
- Students will state the requirements for the position of president.
- Students will identify past presidents who they feel were effective leaders who had an impact on the country.

Materials Needed by Students for Completion
- Poster board or large white paper
- Materials for board games (e.g., folders, colored cards)
- Scrapbooking materials
- Paper bags (for puppets)
- Socks (for puppets)
- DVD or VHS recorder (for commercials) ●

Special Notes on the Use of These Menus
This topic has two different menu formats: Meal menu and Tic-Tac-Toe menu. The Meal menu is specifically selected for its meal-oriented, Bloom's-based options, as it is easily broken into manageable bits. The menu can be cut into strips, each strip featuring its own meal, to be given to students. This way, once students have chosen and submitted the breakfast product for grading, they can move on to the lunch strip, and lastly, they can complete the dinner and dessert strips. Because this type of menu is designed to become more advanced as students move through the meals, teachers may choose to provide their students who have special needs with just the meals and save the dessert for enrichment.

The circle menu gives students the opportunity to create a commercial. Although students enjoy producing their own videos, there are often difficulties obtaining the equipment and scheduling the use of the video recorder. The menu can be modified by allowing students to act out their commercials (like a play), or if students have the technology, they may wish to produce a webcam or Flash version of their commercials.

Time Frame

- 2–3 weeks—Students are given the menus as the unit is started. As the teacher presents lessons throughout the week, he or she should refer back to the menu options associated with that content. The teacher will go over all of the options for that content and have students place check marks in the boxes that represent the activities they are most interested in completing. If students are using the Tic-Tac-Toe menu form, activities chosen and completed should make a column or row. If students are using the Meal menu form, students will complete one product from each meal, with dessert being an optional enrichment product. When students complete these patterns, they will have completed one activity from each content area, learning style, or level of Bloom's Revised taxonomy.
- 1 week—At the start of the unit, the teacher chooses the three activities he or she feels are most valuable for students. Stations can be set up in the classroom. These three activities are available for student choice throughout the week as regular instruction takes place.
- 1–2 days—The teacher chooses an activity from the menu to use with the entire class.

Suggested Forms

- All-purpose rubric
- Oral presentation rubric
- Oral presentation feedback form
- Free-choice proposal form

Our Country's Presidents

Directions: Choose one activity each for breakfast, lunch, and dinner. Dessert is an activity you can choose to do after you have finished your other meals. All products must be completed by: _____.

Breakfast

❏ Design a board game that takes players through the steps needed to become President of the United States.

❏ Select someone famous who has the qualifications to be President but who would probably never run. Make a campaign advertisement for your candidate detailing his or her qualifications.

❏ Free choice—Submit a free-choice proposal about what it takes to be President to your teacher for approval.

Lunch

❏ Choose the President who you feel has had the greatest impact on your state. Perform a song or rap that shares the qualities the President exhibited.

❏ Create a brochure detailing the qualities needed to be an effective President and leader. Include examples from past Presidents to prove your point.

❏ Create a "perfect President puppet" to discuss what it takes to be an effective President. Your puppet can be based on a real President, or you can create your own with characteristics from many different Presidents.

Dinner

❏ Choose a President who you feel is not as well known as he should be considering his contributions to the development of the country. Make an acrostic for the first and last name of the President. Include information about the work he did for each letter of his name.

❏ Choose the President who you feel has had the greatest impact (either positive or negative) on the development of the United States. Come to class as that President and talk about your impact on the country.

❏ Choose the President you think has played the smallest role in American history. Design a scrapbook to reflect his life before and during his time as President. Be sure to include how he impacted the country during his term!

Dessert

❏ Not everyone feels the same about the qualities a President needs to be effective. Design a survey to find out what qualities other people feel are important. After conducting the survey, share your information with your classmates through an oral presentation.

❏ You have decided to run for President! Design a political advertisement that details your experience and qualifications.

Name:_____ Date:_____ ●

Our Country's Presidents

Directions: Check the boxes you plan to complete. They should form a tic-tac-toe across or down. All products are due by: _____.

☐ *Can I Be President?*	☐ *Qualities of an Effective President*	☐ *Presidents of the Past*
Design a board game that takes players through the steps needed to become President of the United States.	Choose the President who you feel has had the greatest impact on your state. Perform a song or rap that shares the qualities the President exhibited to have such an impact.	Choose the President you think has played the smallest role in American history. Design a scrapbook to reflect his life before, during, and after his time as President. Be sure to include how he impacted the country during his term!
☐ *Presidents of the Past*	☐ **Free Choice: Requirements for Being a U.S. President** (Fill out your proposal form before beginning the free choice!)	☐ *Qualities of an Effective President*
Choose the President who you feel has had the greatest impact (either positive or negative) on the development of the United States. Come to class as that President and talk about your impact on the country.		Create a brochure detailing the qualities needed to be an effective President and leader. Include examples from past Presidents to prove your point.
☐ *Qualities of an Effective President*	☐ *Presidents of the Past*	☐ *Can I Be President?*
Create a "perfect President puppet" to discuss what it takes to be an effective President. Your puppet can be based on a real President, or you can create your own with characteristics from many different Presidents.	Choose a President who you feel is not as well known as he should be considering his contributions to the development of the country. Make an acrostic for the first and last name of the President. Include information about the work he did for each letter of his name.	Select someone famous who has the qualifications to be President but who would probably never run. Make a campaign commercial for your candidate detailing his or her qualifications.

Civil and Equal Rights

20-50-80 Menus

Objectives Covered Through These Menus and These Activities
- Students will trace the civil rights and equal rights movements in the 20th century.
- Students will identify key leaders and the roles they played in the civil rights and equal rights movements.

Materials Needed by Students for Completion
- Poster board or large white paper
- Blank index cards (for trading cards)
- Scrapbooking materials ●
- Internet access (for WebQuests)

Special Notes on the Use of These Menus
These menus allow students to create a WebQuest. There are multiple versions and templates for WebQuests available on the Internet. Teachers should decide whether to specify a certain format or allow students to create one of their own choosing.

Time Frame
- 1–2 weeks—Students are given the menus as the unit is started, and the teacher discusses all of the product options on the menus. As the different options are discussed, students will choose products that add to a total of 100 points. As the lessons progress, the teacher and students refer back to the menu options associated with the content being taught.
- 1–2 days—The teacher chooses an activity or product from the menu to use with the entire class.

Suggested Forms
- All-purpose rubric
- Oral presentation rubric
- Student feedback rubric
- Point-based free-choice proposal form

Civil and Equal Rights

Directions: Choose at least two activities from the menu below. The activities must total at least 100 points. Place a check mark next to each box to show which activities you will complete. All activities must be completed by: _____.

20 Points

❐ Create an acrostic for the last name of a leader in the civil rights or equal rights movements. Choose descriptive phrases that highlight the roles he or she played in one of the movements.

❐ Create a set of trading cards for at least eight people who had an impact on the progression of the civil rights or equal rights movements.

50 Points

❐ Create Three Facts and a Fib for a civil rights or equal rights leader of your choice.

❐ Design a civil rights or equal rights persuasive brochure in which you share your thoughts and persuade others to support them.

❐ Make a Venn diagram to compare and contrast the concepts of civil rights and equal rights. Include examples and people in your diagram.

❐ Free choice—Prepare a proposal form and submit your idea for approval.

80 Points

❐ Develop a You Be the Person presentation in which you come to class as a key leader in the civil rights or equal rights movements. Be prepared to share and defend your beliefs, as well as answer questions.

❐ Research how people's rights have changed over the centuries. Design a WebQuest that shows how civil rights or equal rights have changed throughout the history of the United States.

Civil and Equal Rights

Directions: Choose at least two activities from the menu below. The activities must total at least 100 points. Place a check mark next to each box to show which activities you will complete. All activities must be completed by: _____.

---

20 Points

❐ Create an acrostic for the first and last name of a leader in the civil rights or equal rights movements. Choose descriptive phrases that highlight the roles he or she played in one of the movements.

❐ Create a set of trading cards for at least 10 people who had an impact on the progression of the civil rights or equal rights movements.

---

50 Points

❐ Create Three Facts and a Fib for a civil rights or equal rights leader of your choice.

❐ Design a civil rights or equal rights persuasive brochure in which you share your thoughts and persuade others to support them.

❐ Create a scrapbook for a key leader in the civil rights or equal rights movements. Include information about the person's history that may have led to their desire to be a civil rights leader.

❐ Free choice—Prepare a proposal form and submit your idea for approval.

---

80 Points

❐ There have been many famous speeches throughout history, including many related to civil rights. Research and locate a speech about equal rights which you feel should be just as well known. Come to class as the person who gave the speech and read the important passages to your classmates. Be prepared to answer any questions about your speech.

❐ Research how people's rights have changed over the centuries. Design a WebQuest that shows how civil rights or equal rights have changed throughout the development and history of the United States.

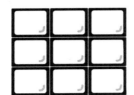

Historical Documents

Game Show Menus

Objectives Covered Through These Menus and These Activities

- Students will evaluate the importance of various historical documents that were written during America's quest for independence.
- Students will evaluate the Articles of Confederation and compare it to the U.S. Constitution.
- Students will analyze the Bill of Rights and the amendments to the U.S. Constitution and the impact these have on their lives.

Materials Needed by Students for Completion

- Poster board or large white paper
- Materials for three-dimensional timelines
- Coat hangers (for mobiles)
- Blank index cards (for mobiles and trading cards)
- String (for mobiles)
- Materials for museum exhibits (e.g., boxes, cards)
- Newspapers
- Paper bags (for puppets) ▲
- Socks (for puppets) ▲
- DVD or VHS recorder (for news reports and informational videos) ●
- Microsoft PowerPoint or other slideshow software

Special Notes on the Use of These Menus

The circle menu gives students the opportunity to create an informational video or news report. Although students enjoy producing their own videos, there are often difficulties obtaining the equipment and scheduling the use of the video recorder. The menus can be modified by allowing students to act out their videos or news reports (like a play), or if students have the technology, they may wish to produce a webcam or Flash version of their products.

Time Frame

- 2–3 weeks—Students are given the menus as the unit is started, and the guidelines and point expectations are discussed. As lessons are taught throughout the unit, students and the teacher can refer back to the options associated with the topic. The teacher will go over all of the options for the topic being covered and will have students place check marks in the boxes next to the activities they are most interested in completing. As teaching continues throughout the 2–3 weeks, activities are discussed, chosen, and submitted for grading.

- 1 week—At the beginning of the unit, the teacher chooses an activity from each area that he or she feels would be most valuable for students. Stations can be set up in the classroom. These activities are available for student choice throughout the week as regular instruction takes place.
- 1–2 days—The teacher chooses an activity from an objective to use with the entire class during lesson time.

Suggested Forms

- All-purpose rubric
- Oral presentation rubric
- Student feedback rubric
- Point-based free-choice proposal form

Guidelines for the Historical Documents Game Show Menu

- You must choose at least one activity from each topic area.
- You may not do more than two activities in any one topic area for credit. (You are, of course, welcome to do more than two for your own investigation.)
- Grading will be ongoing, so turn in products as you complete them.
- All free-choice proposals must be turned in and approved *prior* to working on that free-choice product.
- You must earn 120 points for a 100%. You may earn extra credit up to _____ points.
- You must show your teacher your plan for completion by: _____.

Historical Documents

Declaration of Independence	Articles of Confederation	Constitution	Bill of Rights	Amendments	Points for Each Level
☐ Make a mobile that shows the ideas expressed in the Declaration of Independence. (10 pts.)	☐ Design a set of trading cards for each article and its importance in the Articles of Confederation. (15 pts.)	☐ Create a three-dimensional timeline that shows the major events that led up to the signing of the Constitution. (15 pts.)	☐ Make a Bill of Rights windowpane to share information about each amendment. Be sure to include a drawing for each. (10 pts.)	☐ Create a PowerPoint presentation that shows the rights and freedoms expressed in the amendments to the Constitution. (15 pts.)	10–15 points
☐ Select the most important pieces of the Declaration of Independence and turn them into a song that could have been sung at the time. (25 pts.)	☐ Design a Venn diagram to compare and contrast the information presented in the Articles of Confederation and the U.S. Constitution. (25 pts.)	☐ Develop Three Facts and a Fib about the information contained in the Constitution. (25 pts.)	☐ Create a folded quiz book to quiz your classmates on their knowledge of the Bill of Rights. (20 pts.)	☐ The National Historical Museum has requested that you create a museum exhibit about the amendments that have been added to the Bill of Rights. (25 pts.)	20–25 points
☐ You have been asked to represent your state and sign the newly developed Declaration of Independence. Write an editorial for the newspaper to explain why someone may not want to sign this document. (30 pts.)	☐ Choose one of the delegates who gathered in Philadelphia and create a journal for his experience during the debates before the articles were signed. (30 pts.)	☐ Create a puppet of someone who signed the Constitution. Have your puppet discuss the importance of the document and how it could affect people hundreds of years from now. (30 pts.)	☐ As a newspaper writer, you have been asked to interview the first author of the Bill of Rights. Develop a set of questions you would like to have answered and create realistic answers. (30 pts.)	☐ Prepare a speech about the amendment that you feel is the most important. Your speech will share examples of the guaranteed right(s) found in that amendment and why you feel it is the most important. (30 pts.)	30 points
Free Choice (prior approval) (25–50 pts.)	**Free Choice** (prior approval) (25–50 pts.)	**Free Choice** (prior approval) (25–50 pts.)	**Free Choice** (prior approval) (25–50 pts.)	**Free Choice** (prior approval) (25–50 pts.)	25–50 points
Total:	**Total:**	**Total:**	**Total:**	**Total:**	**Total Grade:**

Historical Documents

Name:_____ Date:_____

Declaration of Independence	Articles of Confederation	Constitution	Bill of Rights	Amendments	Points for Each Level
☐ Make a mobile that shows the ideas expressed in the Declaration of Independence. (10 pts.)	☐ Design a set of trading cards for each article and its importance in the Articles of Confederation. (15 pts.)	☐ Create a three-dimensional timeline that shows the major events that led up to the signing of the Constitution. (10 pts.)	☐ Create a folded quiz book to quiz your classmates on their knowledge of the Bill of Rights. Include real-life examples of the rights and freedoms in some of your questions. (15 pts.)	☐ Create a PowerPoint presentation that shows the rights and freedoms expressed in the amendments to the Constitution. (15 pts.)	10–15 points
☐ Select the most important pieces of the Declaration of Independence and turn them into a song that could have been sung at the time. (25 pts.)	☐ Design a Venn diagram to compare and contrast the information presented in the Articles of Confederation and the U.S. Constitution. (20 pts.)	☐ Develop Three Facts and a Fib about the information contained in the Constitution. (20 pts.)	☐ The National Historical Museum has requested that you create a museum exhibit about the Bill of Rights and its impact on the United States throughout the years. (25 pts.)	☐ Prepare a speech about the amendment that you feel is the most important. Your speech will share examples of the guaranteed right(s) found in that amendment and why you feel it is the most important. (25 pts.)	20–25 points
☐ People your age often consider declaring independence from their parents. Consider your reasons and outline your own Declaration of Independence. Follow the same format as the 1776 Declaration of Independence. (30 pts.)	☐ Create and perform a news report that documents the long days of debate when the delegates gathered in Philadelphia to discuss the effectiveness of the Articles of Confederacy. (30 pts.)	☐ Although written many years ago, the Constitution still has impact on Americans of all ages. Design an informational video on the Constitution and its importance to people your age. (30 pts.)	☐ As a newspaper writer, you have been asked to interview the first author of the Bill of Rights. Develop a set of questions you would like to have answered and create realistic answers. (30 pts.)	☐ Search through the newspaper and locate at least two examples of rights in action that would not have been allowed had additional amendments not been added to the Constitution. Choose one of the two examples to develop into a play for your classmates. (30 pts.)	30 points
Free Choice (prior approval) (25–50 pts.)	**Free Choice** (prior approval) (25–50 pts.)	**Free Choice** (prior approval) (25–50 pts.)	**Free Choice** (prior approval) (25–50 pts.)	**Free Choice** (prior approval) (25–50 pts.)	25–50 points
Total:	Total:	Total:	Total:	Total:	Total Grade:

My Amendment in Depth

Meal Menu ▲ and Tic-Tac-Toe Menu ●

Objectives Covered Through These Menus and These Activities

- Students will state their chosen amendment and be able to interpret its meaning.
- Students will share the history behind their amendment and its development.
- Students will be able to defend the importance of their amendment.

Materials Needed by Students for Completion

- Poster board or large white paper
- Materials for bulletin board displays ●
- Blank index cards (for trading cards) ▲
- Rulers (for comic strips) ▲
- Materials for three-dimensional timelines
- Scrapbooking materials
- Microsoft PowerPoint or other slideshow software

Special Notes on the Use of These Menus

This topic has two different menu formats: Meal menu and Tic-Tac-Toe menu. The Meal menu is specifically selected for its meal-oriented, Bloom's-based options, as it is easily broken into manageable bits. The menu can be cut into strips, each strip featuring its own meal, to be given to students. This way, once students have chosen and submitted the breakfast product for grading, they can move on to the lunch strip, and lastly, they can complete the dinner and dessert strips. Because this type of menu is designed to become more advanced as students move through the meals, teachers may choose to provide their students who have special needs with just the meals and save the dessert for enrichment.

The circle menu allows students to create a bulletin board display. Some classrooms may only have one bulletin board, so the teacher can divide the board into sections, or additional classroom wall or hall space can be sectioned off for the creation of these displays. Students can plan their displays based on the amount of space they are assigned.

Time Frame

- 2–3 weeks—Students are given the menus as the unit is started. As the teacher presents lessons throughout the week, he or she should refer back to the menu options associated with that content. The teacher will go over all of the options for that content and have students place check marks in the boxes that represent the activities they are most interested in completing. If students are using the Tic-Tac-Toe menu form, activities chosen and completed should make a column or row. If students are using the Meal menu form, students will complete one product from each meal, with dessert being an optional enrichment product. When students complete these patterns, they will have completed one activity from each content area, learning style, or level of Bloom's Revised taxonomy.
- 1 week—At the start of the unit, the teacher chooses the three activities he or she feels are most valuable for students. Stations can be set up in the classroom. These three activities are available for student choice throughout the week as regular instruction takes place.
- 1–2 days—The teacher chooses an activity from the menu to use with the entire class.

Suggested Forms

- All-purpose rubric
- Free-choice proposal form

My Amendment in Depth

Directions: Choose one activity each for breakfast, lunch, and dinner. Dessert is an activity you can choose to do after you have finished your other meals. All products must be completed by: _____.

My Amendment is _____. It states _____

_____ .

Breakfast

❏ Design a poster that shows examples of your amendment and its meaning.

❏ Create Three Facts and a Fib about your amendment and what it means to Americans.

❏ Create a set of trading cards for five people. Include people who worked on your amendment and those who benefited from its being ratified.

Lunch

❏ Create a three-dimensional timeline that shows the events that led to the development and ratification of your amendment.

❏ Create a comic strip that shares the main events which led up to the ratification of your amendment.

❏ Pretend your amendment has not been ratified yet. Make an advertisement to convince people of why it should be ratified.

Dinner

❏ Create a scrapbook with at least three recent examples of your amendment at work. If you cannot find recent sources, choose significant historical examples and include why recent examples are not available.

❏ A book is being written about your amendment and its importance to our society today. Create a book cover for this book. Be creative with its title and summary.

❏ Free choice—Submit a free-choice proposal about the importance of your amendment to your teacher for approval.

Dessert

❏ Most amendments are submitted and ratified to solve a problem. Research the history behind your amendment's ratification and create a PowerPoint presentation to share with your classmates.

❏ Write and perform a play about how your life and others' lives would be different if your amendment had not been ratified.

My Amendment in Depth

Directions: Check the boxes you plan to complete. They should form a tic-tac-toe across or down. All products are due by: _____.

My Amendment is _____. It states _____
_____ .

☐ *Meaning*	☐ *Importance*	☐ *History*
Design a poster that shows examples of your amendment and its meaning.	Create a scrapbook with at least five recent examples of your amendment at work. If you cannot find recent sources, choose significant historical examples and include why recent examples are not available.	Most amendments are submitted and ratified to address a problem. Research the history behind your amendment's ratification and create a PowerPoint presentation to share with your classmates.
☐ *History*	☐ **Free Choice: The Meaning of My Amendment** (Fill out your proposal form before beginning the free choice!)	☐ *Importance*
Create a bulletin board display that shares the main events which lead up to the ratification of your amendment.		Write and perform a play about how your life and others' lives would be different if your amendment had not been ratified.
☐ *Importance*	☐ *History*	☐ *Meaning*
A book is being written about your amendment and its importance to our society today. Create a book cover for this book. Be creative with its title and summary.	Create a three-dimensional timeline that shows the events that led to the development and ratification of your amendment.	Create Three Facts and a Fib about your amendment and what it means to Americans.

CHAPTER 6

U.S. History

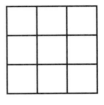

Explorers

Meal Menu ▲ and Tic-Tac-Toe Menu ●

Objectives Covered Through This Menu and These Activities

- Students will recognize the importance and impact of various explorers.
- Students will understand the reasons why explorers made their journeys.

Materials Needed by Students for Completion

- Poster board or large white paper
- Materials for three-dimensional timeline
- Microsoft PowerPoint or other slideshow software
- Materials for trophy
- DVD or VHS recorder (for news reports) ▲ (dessert only)
- Materials for board games (e.g., folders, colored cards)

Special Notes on the Use of This Menu

This topic has two different menu formats: Meal menu and Tic-Tac-Toe menu. The Meal menu is specifically selected for its meal-oriented, Bloom's-based options, as it is easily broken into manageable bits. The menu can be cut into strips, each strip featuring its own meal, to be given to students. This way, once students have chosen and submitted the breakfast product for grading, they can move on to the lunch strip, and lastly, they can complete the dinner and dessert strips. Because this type of menu is designed to become more advanced as students move through the meals, teachers may choose to provide their students who have special needs with just the meals and save the dessert for enrichment.

The triangle menu give students the opportunity to create a news report. Although students enjoy producing their own videos, there are often difficulties obtaining the equipment and scheduling the use of the video recorder. The menus can be modified by allowing students to act out their news reports (like a play), or if students have the technology, they may wish to produce a webcam or Flash version of their news reports.

Time Frame

- 2–3 weeks—Students are given the menus as the unit is started. As the teacher presents lessons throughout the week, he or she should refer back to the menu options associated with that content. The teacher will go over all of the options for that content and have students place check marks in the boxes that represent the activities they are most interested in completing. If students are using the Tic-Tac-Toe menu form, activities chosen and completed should make a column or row. If students are using the Meal menu form, students will complete one product from each meal, with dessert being an optional enrichment product. When students complete these patterns, they will have completed one activity from each content area, learning style, or level of Bloom's Revised taxonomy.
- 1 week—At the start of the unit, the teacher chooses the three activities he or she feels are most valuable for students. Stations can be set up in the classroom. These three activities are available for student choice throughout the week as regular instruction takes place.
- 1–2 days—The teacher chooses an activity from the menu to use with the entire class.

Suggested Forms

- All-purpose rubric
- Oral presentation rubric
- Student feedback rubric
- Free-choice proposal form

Explorers

Directions: Choose one activity each for breakfast, lunch, and dinner. Dessert is an activity you can choose to do after you have finished your other meals. All products must be completed by: _____.

Breakfast

❑ Create a three-dimensional timeline to document the life and adventures of the explorer you are studying.

❑ Create a board game for your explorer's life and adventures. Your game should cover all the major events in your explorer's life, as well as those of his or her explorations.

❑ Design a children's book that shares information about your explorer and his or her pre-journey life.

Lunch

❑ Explorers rarely venture out alone; they need to recruit others to assist in various ways. Design a recruitment brochure explaining the proposed journey and the reasons why this journey is important.

❑ Research the various reasons explorers leave home and venture forth. Create a PowerPoint presentation that discusses these various reasons, as well as reasons specific to your explorer.

❑ Consider the various reasons behind your explorer's adventure. Create a persuasive poster with all of the reasons to support his or her adventure.

Dinner

❑ Create a play in which your explorer visits present time. What would he or she say about his or her impact on the world as it is now?

❑ Your explorer has been nominated to receive the World-Famous Explorer Award. Create a trophy for your explorer based on his or her work and give an acceptance speech as the person talking about his or her impact on today's world.

❑ Free choice—Submit a free-choice proposal about what your explorer would think about our world today to your teacher for approval.

Dessert

❑ Imagine what your explorer would think about the impact his or her journeys have had on the world as it is today. Prepare a You Be the Person presentation in which you come to class as your explorer and share his or her views on the part he or she played in history.

❑ Write and perform a news report that details the work and adventures of your explorer and his or her impact on present-day life.

Explorers

Directions: Check the boxes you plan to complete. They should form a tic-tac-toe across or down. All products are due by: _____.

☐ *What Did They Do?* Create a three-dimensional timeline to document the life and adventures of the explorer you are studying.	☐ *What Would They Think?* Your explorer has been nominated to receive the World-Famous Explorer Award. Create a trophy for your explorer based on his or her work and give an acceptance speech as the person talking about his or her impact on today's world.	☐ *Why Would They Do It?* Explorers rarely venture out alone; they need to recruit others to assist in various ways. Design a recruitment brochure explaining the proposed journey and the reasons why this journey is important.
☐ *Why Would They Do It?* Research the various reasons explorers leave home and venture forth. Create a PowerPoint presentation that discusses these various reasons, as well as reasons specific to your explorer.	☐ **Free Choice: The Life and Adventures of Your Explorer** (Fill out your proposal form before beginning the free choice!)	☐ *What Would They Think?* Write a newspaper article that details the work and adventures of your explorer and his or her impact on present-day life.
☐ *What Would They Think?* Create a play in which your explorer visits present time. What would he or she say about his or her impact on the world as it is now?	☐ *Why Would They Do It?* Consider the various reasons behind your explorer's adventure. Create a persuasive poster with all of the reasons to support his or her adventure.	☐ *What Did They Do?* Create a board game for your explorer's life and adventures. Your game should cover all of the major events in your explorer's life, as well as those in his or her explorations.

The Mayflower Compact

20-50-80 Menus

Objectives Covered Through These Menus and These Activities
- Students will communicate the importance of the Mayflower Compact and its impact on other historical documents.
- Students will state the provisions of the Mayflower Compact.

Materials Needed by Students for Completion
- Poster board or large white paper
- Microsoft PowerPoint or other slideshow software
- Large lined index cards (for instruction cards) ▲
- DVD or VHS recorder (for news reports) ●

Special Notes on the Use of These Menus
The circle menu gives students the opportunity to create a news report. Although students enjoy producing their own videos, there are often difficulties obtaining the equipment and scheduling the use of the video recorder. The menus can be modified by allowing students to act out their news reports (like a play), or if students have the technology, they may wish to produce a webcam or Flash version of their news reports.

Time Frame
- 1–2 weeks—Students are given the menus as the unit is started, and the teacher discusses all of the product options on the menus. As the different options are discussed, students will choose products that add to a total of 100 points. As the lessons progress, the teacher and students refer back to the menu options associated with the content being taught.
- 1–2 days—The teacher chooses an activity or product from the menu to use with the entire class.

Suggested Forms
- All-purpose rubric
- Point-based free-choice proposal form
- Oral presentation rubric
- Student feedback rubric

The Mayflower Compact

Directions: Choose at least two activities from the menu below. The activities must total at least 100 points. Place a check mark next to each box to show which activities you will complete. All activities must be completed by: _____.

---

20 Points

❑ Create a poster that shares the reasons behind the creation of the Mayflower Compact and its importance to the Pilgrims.

❑ Create Three Facts and a Fib about the Mayflower Compact.

---

50 Points

❑ Rewrite the Mayflower Compact in words your classmates would understand. Then create a PowerPoint presentation to share your translated version.

❑ Design an advertisement for a new book about the Mayflower Compact and its impact on the new government in the Americas.

❑ Create an instruction card that explains how to be a good citizen based on the Mayflower Compact.

❑ Free choice—Prepare a proposal form and submit your idea for approval.

---

80 Points

❑ Create a Pilgrim game show in which Pilgrim contestants are asked to determine if the Mayflower Compact would support various situations.

❑ Write a children's book about life in the New World, the development of the Mayflower Compact, and its impact on the Pilgrims.

The Mayflower Compact

Directions: Choose at least two activities from the menu below. The activities must total at least 100 points. Place a check mark next to each box to show which activities you will complete. All activities must be completed by: _____.

---

20 Points

❑ Create a brochure that shares the reasons behind the creation of the Mayflower Compact and its importance to the Pilgrims.

❑ Create Three Facts and a Fib about the Mayflower Compact.

---

50 Points

❑ Rewrite the Mayflower Compact in words your classmates would understand. Then create a PowerPoint presentation to share your translated version.

❑ Design a book cover for a new book about the Mayflower Compact and its impact on the development of the U.S. Constitution.

❑ Write a song about the Mayflower Compact and what it meant to the Pilgrims' lives.

❑ Free choice—Prepare a proposal form and submit your idea for approval.

---

80 Points

❑ Create a news report about the signing of the Mayflower Compact. Be sure to interview at least two people this document will impact and their thoughts on its signing.

❑ Create a Pilgrim game show in which Pilgrim contestants are asked to determine if the Mayflower Compact would support various situations.

The Revolutionary War

List Menus

Objectives Covered Through These Menus and These Activities

- Students will analyze the causes of the American Revolution.
- Students will explain the roles played by significant individuals during the American Revolution.
- Students will explain the issues surrounding important events of the American Revolution.

Materials Needed by Students for Completion

- Poster board or large white paper
- Materials for three-dimensional timelines
- Blank index cards (for trading cards)
- DVD or VHS recorder (for news reports and commercials)
- Internet access (for WebQuests)
- Rulers (for comic strips)
- Paper bags (for puppets)
- Socks (for puppets)
- Scrapbooking materials
- Materials for quiz boards (e.g., batteries, holiday lights, aluminum foil, tape)
- Product cube template
- Materials for dioramas (e.g., shoe boxes, cards)

Special Notes on the Use of These Menus

These menus offer students the opportunity to create a quiz board. Quiz boards can range from simple to very complex, depending on the knowledge and ability of the student. Quiz boards work best when the teacher creates a "tester" that can be used to check any boards that are submitted. Basic instructions on how to create quiz boards and testers can be found at http://www.cesiscience.org/attachments/article/100/QuizBoardDirections.pdf.

These menus also allow students to create a WebQuest. There are multiple versions and templates for WebQuests available on the Internet. Teachers should decide whether to specify a certain format or allow students to create one of their own choosing.

These menus give students the opportunity to create a news report or commercial. Although students enjoy producing their own videos, there are often difficulties obtaining the equipment and scheduling the use of the video recorder. The menus can be modified by allowing students to act out their news reports or commercials (like a play), or if students have the technology, they may wish to produce a webcam or Flash version of their news reports or commercials.

Time Frame

- 1–2 weeks—Students are given the menus as the unit is started, and guidelines and point expectations are discussed. Students will usually need to earn 100 points for 100%, although there is an opportunity for extra credit if the teacher would like to use another target number. Because these menus cover one topic in depth, the teacher will go over all of the options on the menus and have students place check marks in the boxes next to the activities they are most interested in completing. Teachers will need to set aside a few moments with each student to sign the agreement at the bottom of the page. As instruction continues, activities are completed by students and submitted for grading.
- 1–2 days—The teacher chooses an activity or product from an objective to use with the entire class during lesson time.

Suggested Forms

- All-purpose rubric
- Point-based free-choice proposal form
- Oral presentation rubric
- Student feedback rubric

The Revolutionary War: Side 1

Guidelines:

1. You may complete as many of the activities listed as you can within the time period.
2. You may choose any combination of activities.
3. Your goal is 100 points. You may earn up to _____ points extra credit.
4. You may be as creative as you like within the guidelines listed below.
5. You must show your plan to your teacher by _____.
6. Activities may be turned in at any time during the working time period. They will be graded and recorded on this sheet as you continue to work, so keep it safe!

Plan to Do	Activity to Complete (Side 1: 15–25 points)	Point Value	Date Completed	Points Earned
	Create a set of trading cards for the people who played major roles in the events leading up to the war and during the war itself.	15		
	Design a cube that shares the events that led up to the war.	15		
	Write Three Facts and a Fib about the events that led up to the Revolutionary War.	20		
	Create a diorama of the most significant event that led up to the Revolutionary War.	25		
	Create a quiz board for the significant individuals who participated in the war.	25		
	Create a Venn diagram that compares and contrasts the qualities of the colonies before and after the Revolutionary War.	25		
	Design a comic strip that details the communications between the colonies and King George III before the war.	25		
	Design a Revolutionary War scrapbook that covers the major events during the war.	25		
	Design a three-dimensional timeline with the significant events of the Revolutionary War.	25		
	Total number of points you are planning to earn from Side 1.	**Total points earned from Side 1:**		

The Revolutionary War: Side 2

Plan to Do	Activity to Complete (Side 2: 30 points and up)	Point Value	Date Completed	Points Earned
	Create a news report from the most important event in the war describing what is happening, why it is happening, and why this could be the most important event of the war.	30		
	Create a newspaper article that could have appeared in an English newspaper that details the events that led up to the Revolutionary War.	30		
	Interview one of the people who played a significant role in the American Revolution. Focus on the reasons behind his or her actions.	30		
	Create a commercial that loyalists could have used to support their cause.	35		
	Create a Patriot and a King George III puppet and perform a puppet show in which they share their opinions about the colonies.	35		
	Create a WebQuest for the major battles in the Revolutionary War. Include present-day as well as historical information about these locations.	35		
	Free choice: must be outlined on a proposal form and approved before beginning work.	10–40 points		
	Total number of points you are planning to earn from Side 1.	**Total points earned from Side 1:**		
	Total number of points you are planning to earn from Side 2.	**Total points earned from Side 2:**		
		Grand Total (/100)		

I am planning to complete _____ activities that could earn up to a total of _____ points.

Teacher's initials _____ Student's signature _____

Name:_____ Date:_____ ●

The Revolutionary War: Side 1

Guidelines:
1. You may complete as many of the activities listed as you can within the time period.
2. You may choose any combination of activities.
3. Your goal is 100 points. You may earn up to _____ points extra credit.
4. You may be as creative as you like within the guidelines listed below.
5. You must show your plan to your teacher by _____.
6. Activities may be turned in at any time during the working time period. They will be graded and recorded on this sheet as you continue to work, so keep it safe!

Plan to Do	Activity to Complete (Side 1: 15–25 points)	Point Value	Date Completed	Points Earned
	Create a set of trading cards for the people who played major roles in the events leading up to the war and during the war itself.	15		
	Create a quiz board for the significant individuals who participated in the war.	15		
	Design a cube that shares the events that led up to the war.	15		
	Design a three-dimensional timeline with the significant events of the Revolutionary War.	15		
	Create a diorama of the most significant event that led up to the Revolutionary War.	20		
	Create a Venn diagram that compares and contrasts the qualities of the colonies before and after the Revolutionary War.	20		
	Design a comic strip that details the communications between the colonies and King George III before the war.	20		
	Write Three Facts and a Fib about the events that led up to the Revolutionary War.	20		
	Design a Revolutionary War scrapbook that covers the major events during the war.	25		
	Total number of points you are planning to earn from Side 1.	**Total points earned from Side 1:**		

The Revolutionary War: Side 2

Plan to Do	Activity to Complete (Side 2: 30 points and up)	Point Value	Date Completed	Points Earned
	Create a WebQuest for the major battles in the Revolutionary War. Include present-day as well as historical information about these locations.	30		
	Create a Patriot and a King George III puppet and perform a puppet show in which they share their opinions about the colonies.	30		
	Interview one of the people who played a significant role in the American Revolution. Focus on the reasons behind his or her actions.	30		
	Create a news report from the most important event in the war describing what is happening, why it is happening, and why this could be the most important event of the war.	30		
	Create a newspaper article that could have appeared in an English newspaper that details the events that led up to the Revolutionary War.	30		
	Create a commercial that loyalists could have used to support their cause.	30		
	Free choice: must be outlined on a proposal form and approved before beginning work.	10–40 points		
	Total number of points you are planning to earn from Side 1.	**Total points earned from Side 1:**		
	Total number of points you are planning to earn from Side 2.	**Total points earned from Side 2:**		
		Grand Total (/100)		

I am planning to complete _____ activities that could earn up to a total of _____ points.

Teacher's initials _____ Student's signature _____

Revolutionary War Cube

Complete the cube about the events that led to the Revolutionary War. Each side of the cube should include one event with a short explanation of its impact on the war. Use this pattern or create your own cube.

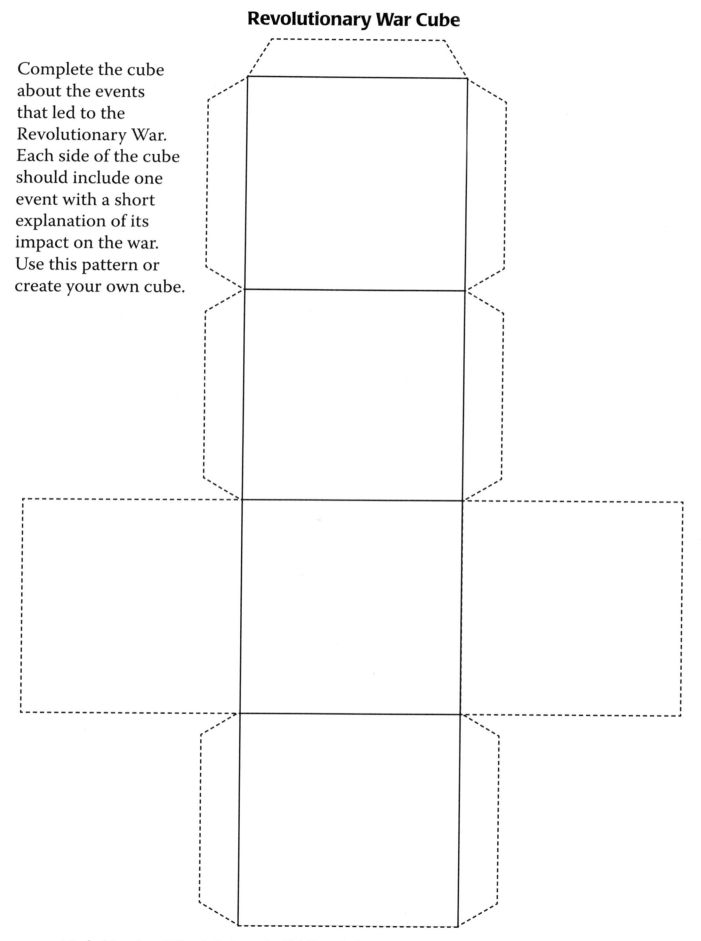

```
20
  ☐ _____
  ☐ _____
50
  ☐ _____
  ☐ _____
  ☐ _____
80
  ☐ _____
  ☐ _____
```

The War of 1812

20-50-80 Menus

Objectives Covered Through These Menus and These Activities
- Students will identify the events that led up to the War of 1812.
- Students will explain the impact of this war and its importance in history.

Materials Needed by Students for Completion
- Materials for board games (e.g., folders, colored cards)
- Microsoft PowerPoint or other slideshow software ▲
- Materials for three-dimensional timelines ●
- Scrapbooking materials ●
- DVD or VHS recorder (for news reports) ●
- "Old Ironsides" by Oliver Wendell Holmes ▲

Special Notes on the Use of These Menus
The circle menus give students the opportunity to create a news report. Although students enjoy producing their own videos, there are often difficulties obtaining the equipment and scheduling the use of the video recorder. The menus can be modified by allowing students to act out their news reports (like a play), or if students have the technology, they may wish to produce a webcam or Flash version of their news reports.

Time Frame
- 1–2 weeks—Students are given the menus as the unit is started, and the teacher discusses all of the product options on the menus. As the different options are discussed, students will choose products that add to a total of 100 points. As the lessons progress, the teacher and students refer back to the menu options associated with the content being taught.
- 1–2 days—The teacher chooses an activity or product from the menu to use with the entire class.

Suggested Forms
- All-purpose rubric
- Point-based free-choice proposal form

The War of 1812

Directions: Choose at least two activities from the menu below. The activities must total at least 100 points. Place a check mark next to each box to show which activities you will complete. All activities must be completed by: _____.

---

20 Points

❏ Create a folded quiz book for the events leading up to the War of 1812.

❏ Design Three Facts and a Fib for the War of 1812.

---

50 Points

❏ Create a board game that takes players through the events leading up to the war, as well as its major battles.

❏ Not all soldiers and sailors who fought in this war did so by choice. Investigate the idea of impressment, and then create a brochure that shares the reasons behind its use.

❏ Using a Venn diagram, compare and contrast the Revolutionary War to the War of 1812.

❏ Free choice—Prepare a proposal form and submit your idea for approval.

---

80 Points

❏ Research the role that the War of 1812 played in the writing of "The Star-Spangled Banner." Write and perform a play that shows the events of the war and their importance in the song's creation.

❏ Read the poem "Old Ironsides" by Oliver Wendell Holmes. Create a PowerPoint presentation that shares the poem, analyzes the meaning of the stanzas, and shows the importance this ship played in the War of 1812.

Name:_____ Date:_____

The War of 1812

Directions: Choose at least two activities from the menu below. The activities must total at least 100 points. Place a check mark next to each box to show which activities you will complete. All activities must be completed by: _____.

---

20 Points

- ❏ Create a three-dimensional timeline for the events leading up to the War of 1812.
- ❏ Design Three Facts and a Fib for the War of 1812.

---

50 Points

- ❏ Create a board game that takes players through the events leading up to the war, as well as its major battles.
- ❏ Not all soldiers and sailors who fought in this war did so by choice. Investigate the idea of impressment, and then create a brochure that shares the reasons behind its use.
- ❏ Choosing either a soldier or sailor, create a scrapbook that details his experiences during the War of 1812.
- ❏ Free choice—Prepare a proposal form and submit your idea for approval.

---

80 Points

- ❏ Research the role that the War of 1812 played in the writing of "The Star-Spangled Banner." Write and perform a play that shows the events of the war and their importance in the song's creation.
- ❏ Choose the most important aspect or event in the War of 1812 and create a live, on-the-spot news report that covers the details of the event.

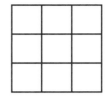

Manifest Destiny

Meal Menu ▲ and Tic-Tac-Toe Menu ●

Objectives Covered Through These Menus and These Activities

- Students will evaluate the idea of Manifest Destiny and its impact on U.S. history.
- Students will determine examples of Manifest Destiny in the past and present.

Materials Needed by Students for Completion

- Microsoft PowerPoint or other slideshow software ●
- Materials for three-dimensional timelines
- Materials for museum exhibits (e.g., boxes, cards) ▲
- Product cube template
- Materials for dioramas (e.g., shoe boxes, cards)

Special Notes on the Use of These Menus

This topic has two different menu formats: Meal menu and Tic-Tac-Toe menu. The Meal menu is specifically selected for its meal-oriented, Bloom's-based options, as it is easily broken into manageable bits. The menu can be cut into strips, each strip featuring its own meal, to be given to students. This way, once students have chosen and submitted the breakfast product for grading, they can move on to the lunch strip, and lastly, they can complete the dinner and dessert strips. Because this type of menu is designed to become more advanced as students move through the meals, teachers may choose to provide their students who have special needs with just the meals and save the dessert for enrichment.

Time Frame

- 2–3 weeks—Students are given the menus as the unit is started. As the teacher presents lessons throughout the week, he or she should refer back to the menu options associated with that content. The teacher will go over all of the options for that content and have students place check marks in the boxes that represent the activities they are most interested in completing. If students are using the Tic-Tac-Toe menu form, activities chosen and completed should make a column or row. If students are using the Meal menu form, students will complete one product from each meal, with dessert being an optional enrichment product. When students complete these patterns, they will have completed one activity from each content area, learning style, or level of Bloom's Revised taxonomy.

- 1 week—At the start of the unit, the teacher chooses the three activities he or she feels are most valuable for students. Stations can be set up in the classroom. These three activities are available for student choice throughout the week as regular instruction takes place.
- 1–2 days—The teacher chooses an activity from the menu to use with the entire class.

Suggested Forms

- All-purpose rubric
- Oral presentation rubric
- Student feedback rubric
- Free-choice proposal form

Manifest Destiny

Directions: Choose one activity each for breakfast, lunch, and dinner. Dessert is an activity you can choose to do after you have finished your other meals. All products must be completed by: _____.

Breakfast

❒ Design a cartoon that either promotes the idea of Manifest Destiny or discourages it.

❒ Create a product cube with drawings that share six different detailed reasons people may choose to venture forth into new areas.

❒ Create a flipbook that shares the reasons why people choose to adventure into new areas. Prioritize your reasons by placing the most common reason on the leftmost flap and the least common reason all the way to the right.

Lunch

❒ Create a three-dimensional timeline for the explorations that made Manifest Destiny a reality.

❒ Create a museum exhibit that shares the events that led up to the great Westward Movement. Be sure to mention the term "Manifest Destiny"!

❒ Design a diorama for the most important event in the Manifest Destiny movement.

Dinner

❒ Manifest Destiny is still at work today, just in different ways. Create a speech that supports this theory with proof that it is happening.

❒ Write a children's book that could teach others about the benefits of Manifest Destiny in today's world. Be sure and include examples!

❒ Free choice—Submit a free-choice proposal about Manifest Destiny to your teacher for approval.

Dessert

❒ Research various examples of artwork created during the 1840s that were used to encourage people to move west. Choose the painting that you think was the most effective in persuading people. Design a brochure that shares the history of the painting and why you felt it was most persuasive.

❒ Consider the name of the movement—Manifest Destiny—and what the words really mean. Do you agree that the name for the movement is appropriate? Create a news article about the meaning of Manifest Destiny and its impact on the areas that were being explored and the explorers.

Name:_____ Date:_____

Manifest Destiny

Directions: Check the boxes you plan to complete. They should form a tic-tac-toe across or down. All products are due by: _____.

☐ *He Said What?* Research John L. O'Sullivan's famous words about Manifest Destiny. Evaluate his statement and create a PowerPoint presentation that shows how the U.S. had pursued its "destiny" through the years beginning with Christopher Columbus.	☐ *Why Go?* Create a product cube with drawings that share six different detailed reasons people may choose to venture forth into new areas.	☐ *Is It Over Yet?* Is Manifest Destiny still at work today? After researching the reasons people choose to move in new directions, decide if this is still occurring. Create a speech that supports your theory with proof that it is not happening, or with examples that it is.
☐ *How Good Could It Get?* Write a children's book that could teach others about the benefits of Manifest Destiny in today's world. Be sure to include examples!	☐ **Free Choice: Manifest Destiny** (Fill out your proposal form before beginning the free choice!)	☐ *Good or Bad Idea?* Consider the name of the movement—Manifest Destiny—and what the words really mean. Do you agree that the name for the movement is appropriate? Create a newspaper article about the meaning of Manifest Destiny and its impact on the areas that were being explored and the explorers.
☐ *Should I Go or Should I Stay?* Design a cartoon that either promotes the idea of Manifest Destiny or discourages it.	☐ *Did Art Impact Your Decision?* Research various examples of artwork created during the 1840s that were used to encourage people to move west. Choose the painting that you think was the most effective in persuading people. Design a brochure that shares the history of the painting and why you felt it was most persuasive.	☐ *When Did It All Start?* Although the term "Manifest Destiny" was not coined until 1839, there were various events that took place to encourage the move westward. Create a three-dimensional timeline for the explorations that made Manifest Destiny a reality.

Manifest Destiny Cube

Complete the cube with drawings that show at least six different detailed reasons why people would choose to venture into new areas. Include historical examples for each reason. Use this pattern or create your own cube.

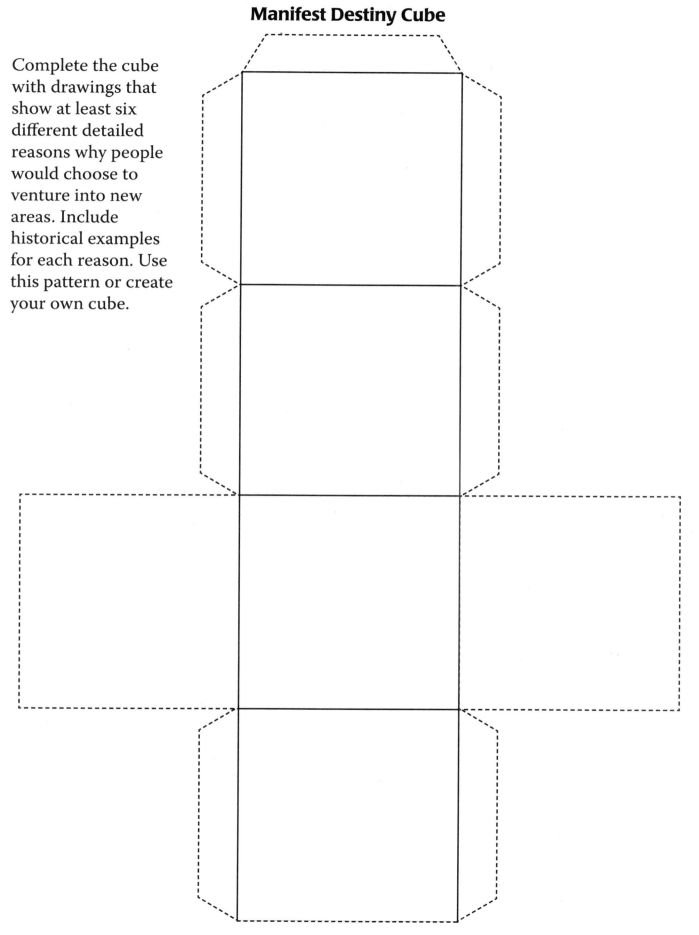

The Mexican-American War

20-50-80 Menus

Objectives Covered Through These Menus and These Activities

- Students will identify the causes of the Mexican-American War.
- Students will evaluate the importance of the events in the Mexican-American War.

Materials Needed by Students for Completion

- Materials for bulletin board displays ●
- Materials for three-dimensional timelines ▲
- Materials for dioramas (e.g., shoe boxes, cards) ▲
- Graph paper or Internet access (for crossword puzzles) ●
- Product cube template ▲

Special Notes on the Use of These Menus

The circle menu allows students to create a bulletin board display. Some classrooms may only have one bulletin board, so the teacher can divide the board into sections, or additional classroom wall or hall space can be sectioned off for the creation of these displays. Students can plan their displays based on the amount of space they are assigned.

Time Frame

- 1–2 weeks—Students are given the menus as the unit is started, and the teacher discusses all of the product options on the menus. As the different options are discussed, students will choose products that add to a total of 100 points. As the lessons progress, the teacher and students refer back to the menu options associated with the content being taught.
- 1–2 days—The teacher chooses an activity or product from the menu to use with the entire class.

Suggested Forms

- All-purpose rubric
- Student-taught lesson rubric
- Point-based free-choice proposal form

The Mexican-American War

Directions: Choose at least two activities from the menu below. The activities must total at least 100 points. Place a check mark next to each box to show which activities you will complete. All activities must be completed by: _____.

---

20 Points

❏ Create a flipbook that shares the causes for the Mexican-American War, as well as the major events during the war.

❏ Create a three-dimensional timeline that shows the events that led to the Mexican-American War.

---

50 Points

❏ Create a diorama for the most important interaction that led to the war, or one that occurred during the war itself.

❏ Complete a Who, What, Where, When, Why, and How cube for the Mexican-American War.

❏ Write an article for a Northern newspaper reporting on what is going to happen now that the Mexican-American War is over.

❏ Free choice—Prepare a proposal form and submit your idea for approval.

---

80 Points

❏ Write a poem on the Mexican-American War from the perspective of a young Texan who has just joined the Union.

❏ Prepare and teach a short class lesson on one of the following: the causes of the war, the events of the war, or the results of the war.

The Mexican-American War

Directions: Choose at least two activities from the menu below. The activities must total at least 100 points. Place a check mark next to each box to show which activities you will complete. All activities must be completed by: _____.

---

20 Points

❏ Create a flipbook that shares the causes for the Mexican-American War, as well as the major events during the war.

❏ Design a bulletin board display that shows the timeline of events that led to the Mexican-American War.

---

50 Points

❏ Create a crossword puzzle about the key events that led up to the Mexican-American War, as well as the famous people involved.

❏ Prepare and teach a short class lesson on one of the following: the causes of the war, the events of the war, or the results of the war.

❏ Write an article for a Northern newspaper reporting on what is going to happen now that the Mexican-American War is over.

❏ Free choice—Prepare a proposal form and submit your idea for approval.

---

80 Points

❏ Write a poem on the Mexican-American War from the perspective of a young Texan who has just joined the Union.

❏ Create a play about a town meeting in which the townspeople debate the boundary dispute.

The Mexican-American War

Complete the cube by answering "Who?" "What?" "Where?" "When?" "Why?" and "How?" to investigate the Mexican-American War. Use this pattern or create your own cube.

The Civil War

List Menu ▲ and Baseball Menu ●

Objectives Covered Through These Menus and These Activities

- Students will understand the causes of the Civil War.
- Students will understand the leaders of the Civil War and the roles they played.
- Students will understand the major events in the Civil War and their impact on the progression of the war.

Materials Needed by Students for Completion

- Poster board or large white paper
- Materials for three-dimensional timelines
- Coat hangers (for mobiles)
- Blank index cards (for mobiles and trading cards)
- String (for mobiles)
- Map of the 13 colonies
- *Mustang Flats* by G. Clifton Wisler
- Materials for board games (e.g., folders, colored cards)
- Microsoft PowerPoint or other slideshow software ▲
- Internet Access (for WebQuests)
- Scrapbooking materials
- Product cube template
- Materials for dioramas (e.g., shoe boxes, cards)

Special Notes on the Use of These Menus

These menus allow students to create a WebQuest. There are multiple versions and templates for WebQuests available on the Internet. Teachers should decide whether to specify a certain format or allow students to create one of their own choosing.

Time Frame

- 2–3 weeks—Students are given the menus as the unit is started, and guidelines and point expectations are discussed. Usually, students are expected to complete 100 points. Because these menus cover one topic in depth, the teacher will go over all of the options for the topic being covered and have students place check marks in the boxes next to the activities they are most interested in completing. As instruction continues, activities are completed by students and submitted for grading.

- 1 week—At the beginning of the unit, the teacher chooses one or two higher level activities that can be integrated into whole-group instruction throughout the week.
- 1–2 days—The teacher chooses an activity from an objective to use with the entire class during lesson time.

Suggested Forms

- All-purpose rubric
- Oral presentation rubric
- Student feedback rubric
- Point-based free-choice proposal form

Name:_____ Date:_____ ▲

The Civil War: Side 1

Guidelines:
1. You may complete as many of the activities listed as you can within the time period.
2. You may choose any combination of activities.
3. Your goal is 100 points. You may earn up to _____ points extra credit.
4. You may be as creative as you like within the guidelines listed below.
5. You must show your plan to your teacher by _____.
6. Activities may be turned in at any time during the working time period. They will be graded and recorded on this sheet as you continue to work, so keep it safe!

Plan to Do	Activity to Complete (Side 1: 15–30 points)	Point Value	Date Completed	Points Earned
	Design a windowpane of "battle terms" that any good soldier should know.	15		
	Create a mobile that shows how various states supported the Civil War.	15		
	Create a set of trading cards for the important leaders associated with the Civil War.	15		
	Using a map of the original 13 states, mark the location of the major battles in the Civil War. Include a color code for the victors.	15		
	Create a pamphlet that shows the components of the U.S. Constitution and the Confederate Constitution; include information about the leaders of each.	20		
	Create a three-dimensional timeline that shows the events leading to the South's secession.	20		
	Create Three Facts and a Fib about one of the leaders in the Civil War.	20		
	Make a cube that shares key information about six of the battles in the Civil War.	20		
	Make a diorama for one of the battles in the Civil War.	20		
	Using a Venn diagram, compare and contrast the Northern and Southern issues prior to the Civil War.	20		
	Create a PowerPoint presentation that compares and contrasts characteristics of the North and South before and after the Civil War.	30		
	Make a board game based on the impact of the Civil War on industry and trade.	30		
	Write a newspaper article chronicling one of the most significant battles during the Civil War.	30		
	Total number of points you are planning to earn from Side 1.		**Total points earned from Side 1:**	

© Prufrock Press Inc. • *Differentiating Instruction With Menus for the Inclusive Classroom: Social Studies* • *Grades 6–8*

The Civil War: Side 2

Plan to Do	Activity to Complete (Side 2: 35 points and up)	Point Value	Date Completed	Points Earned
	Create a WebQuest that takes questors on a virtual field trip to important places related to the Civil War.	35		
	Read *Mustang Flats* by G. Clifton Wisler. Create a flipbook that shows which parts of the story are fact and which are fiction.	40		
	There were many songs from the Civil War time period. Research them and perform one for your classmates.	40		
	Many great artists create paintings that show historical events and their impact on people. Design a mural that could represent the Civil War and its impact on the Northern and Southern states.	40		
	Choose the person you feel had the biggest impact on the war and write a newspaper article about his or her impact and why you feel it was the most significant.	50		
	Create a political cartoon showing the Southern viewpoint of the U.S. Constitution.	50		
	You will be attending the Texas Secession Convention. Prepare to debate your point of view with another participant in the convention.	55		
	Create a scrapbook to document the life of a woman on the home front.	55		
	Create a family scrapbook for a family with two sons, both old enough to fight in the Civil War. This family, like many others, will be split by the war with one of the sons supporting the opposite side of his brother. The scrapbook should include the reason each boy uses to determine the side he will support, his journeys as the war progresses, and the battles in which he finds himself participating. Use statistics to determine the amount of people who did not make it out of each battle and plan your scrapbook accordingly.	100		
	Free choice: must be outlined on a proposal form and approved before beginning work.	10–40 points		
	Total number of points you are planning to earn from Side 1.	**Total points earned from Side 1:**		
	Total number of points you are planning to earn from Side 2.	**Total points earned from Side 2:**		
		Grand Total (/100)		

I am planning to complete _____ activities that could earn up to a total of _____ points.

Teacher's initials _____ Student's signature _____

The Civil War

Directions: Look through the following choices and decide how you want to make your game add to 100 points. Singles are worth 10, Doubles are worth 30, Triples are worth 50, and a Home Run is worth 100. Choose any combination you want! Place a check mark next to each choice you are going to complete. Make sure that your points equal 100!

Singles—10 Points Each

- ❏ Create a three-dimensional timeline that shows the events leading to the South's secession.
- ❏ Design a windowpane of "battle terms" that any good soldier should know.
- ❏ Using a Venn diagram, compare and contrast the issues that the North and South disagreed about prior to the Civil War.
- ❏ Create a pamphlet that shows the components of the U.S. Constitution and the Confederate Constitution; include information about the leaders of each.
- ❏ Create a mobile that shows how various states supported the Civil War.
- ❏ Make a diorama for one of the battles in the Civil War.
- ❏ Create a set of trading cards for the important leaders associated with the Civil War.
- ❏ Make a cube that shares key information about six of the battles in the Civil War.
- ❏ Using a map of the original 13 states, mark the location of the major battles in the Civil War. Include a color code for the victors.
- ❏ Create Three Facts and a Fib about one of the leaders in the Civil War.

Doubles—30 Points Each

- ❏ Interview a Southern plantation owner on his views about secession. Prepare your interview questions and appropriate responses.
- ❏ Read *Mustang Flats* by G. Clifton Wisler. Create a flipbook that shows which parts of the story are fact and which are fiction.
- ❏ Write a newspaper article chronicling one of the most significant battles during the Civil War.
- ❏ Make a board game based on the impact of the Civil War on industry and trade.
- ❏ Create a WebQuest that takes questors on a virtual field trip to important places related to the Civil War.

Doubles—30 Points Each (continued)

❏ There were many songs from the Civil War time period. Research them and perform one for your classmates.

❏ Many great artists create paintings that show historical events and their impact on people. Design a mural that could represent the Civil War and its impact on the Northern and Southern states.

❏ Free choice—Prepare a proposal form and submit your idea for approval.

Triples—50 Points Each

❏ Create a political cartoon showing the Southern viewpoint of the U.S. Constitution.

❏ You have two sons who are getting ready to go fight in the Civil War. They have not decided which army they want to fight for; they just know they want to fight! Unfortunately, you cannot talk them out of it. Write a persuasive letter to your children explaining which side they should choose and why.

❏ You will be attending the Texas Secession Convention. Prepare to debate your point of view with another participant in the convention.

❏ Create a scrapbook to document the life of a woman on the home front.

❏ Choose the person you feel had the biggest impact on the war and write a newspaper article about his or her impact and why you feel it was the most significant.

Home Run—100 Points Each

❏ Create a family scrapbook for a family with three sons, all old enough to fight in the Civil War. This family, like many others, will be split by the war with at least one of the sons supporting the opposite side of his brothers. The scrapbook should include the reason each boy uses to determine the side he will support, his journeys as the war progresses, the leaders he meets, and the battles in which he finds himself participating. Use statistics to determine the amount of people who did not make it out of each battle and plan your scrapbook accordingly.

I Chose:

_____ Singles (10 points each)

_____ Doubles (30 points each)

_____ Triples (50 points each)

_____ Home Run (100 points)

Civil War Cube

After selecting six different important battles in the Civil War, complete each side of the cube with information about the battle and its role in the Civil War. Use this pattern or create your own cube.

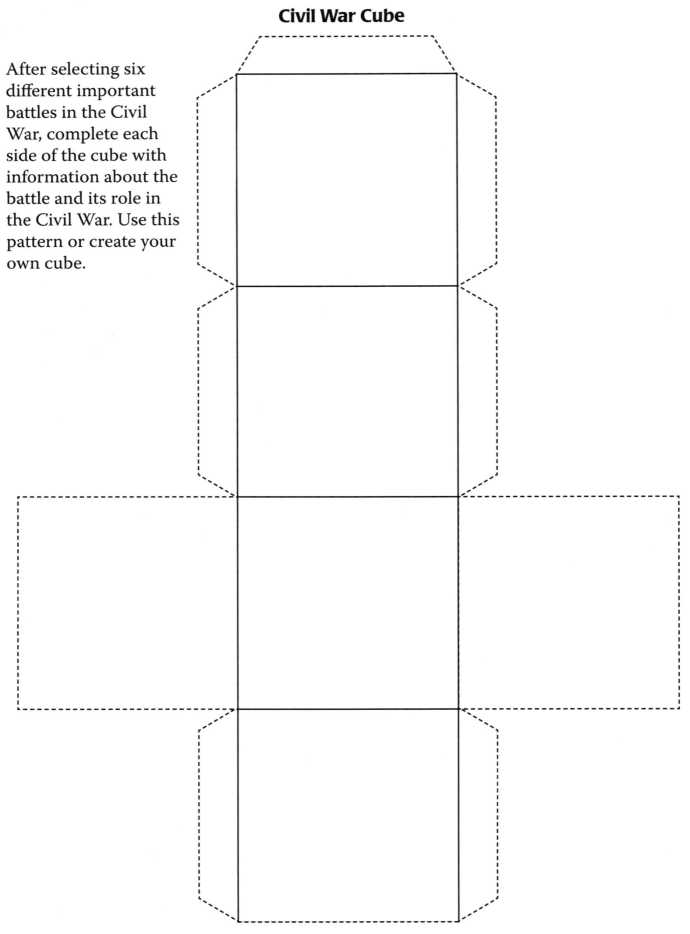

Our State's History

List Menus

Objectives Covered Through These Menus and These Activities
- Students will identity important events in their state's history.
- Students will locate on a map their state's locations of historical importance.
- Students will understand the significance of their state's historical locations.
- Students will determine which leader has had the greatest impact on their state's history.

Materials Needed by Students for Completion
- Poster board or large white paper
- Magazines (for collages)
- Materials for dioramas (e.g., shoe boxes, cards)
- Materials for museum exhibits (e.g., boxes, cards)
- Materials for quiz boards (e.g., batteries, holiday lights, aluminum foil, tape)
- Microsoft PowerPoint or other slideshow software
- Materials for three-dimensional timelines
- Graph paper or Internet access (for crossword puzzles)
- Internet access (for WebQuests)
- Materials for class games

Special Notes on the Use of These Menus
These menus offer students the opportunity to create a quiz board. Quiz boards can range from simple to very complex, depending on the knowledge and ability of the student. Quiz boards work best when the teacher creates a "tester" that can be used to check any boards that are submitted. Basic instructions on how to create quiz boards and testers can be found at http://www.cesiscience.org/attachments/article/100/QuizBoardDirections.pdf.

These menus also give students the opportunity to create a class game. The length of the game is not stated in the product guidelines, so the teacher can determine what works best. It may be a good idea to have students start with shorter games and work up to longer games with a review focus.

These menus allow students to create a WebQuest. There are multiple versions and templates for WebQuests available on the Internet. Teachers should decide whether to specify a certain format or allow students to create one of their own choosing.

Time Frame

- 1–2 weeks—Students are given the menus as the unit is started, and guidelines and point expectations are discussed. Students will usually need to earn 100 points for 100%, although there is an opportunity for extra credit if the teacher would like to use another target number. Because these menus cover one topic in depth, the teacher will go over all of the options on the menus and have students place check marks in the boxes next to the activities they are most interested in completing. Teachers will need to set aside a few moments with each student to sign the agreement at the bottom of the page. As instruction continues, activities are completed by students and submitted for grading.
- 1–2 days—The teacher chooses an activity or product from an objective to use with the entire class during lesson time.

Suggested Forms

- All-purpose rubric
- Oral presentation rubric
- Student feedback rubric
- Student-taught lesson rubric
- Point-based free-choice proposal form

Our State's History: Side 1

Guidelines:
1. You may complete as many of the activities listed as you can within the time period.
2. You may choose any combination of activities.
3. Your goal is 100 points. You may earn up to _____ points extra credit.
4. You may be as creative as you like within the guidelines listed below.
5. You must show your plan to your teacher by _____.
6. Activities may be turned in at any time during the working time period. They will be graded and recorded on this sheet as you continue to work, so keep it safe!

Plan to Do	Activity to Complete (Side 1: 15–25 points)	Point Value	Date Completed	Points Earned
	Complete another student's crossword puzzle.	15		
	Make a flipbook of the important events in your state's history.	15		
	Create a crossword puzzle about your state's history.	20		
	Create a diorama of your state's most important historical location. Include a paragraph about why this location is the most important.	20		
	Design a book cover for a book about your state's history.	20		
	Design a folded flipbook for your state's history and its leaders throughout its history.	20		
	Design an advertisement for one of your state's historical locations.	20		
	Create a collage that shares photos, words, and important information about your state and its history.	20		
	Create a PowerPoint presentation that provides information about the location you feel is most important in your state.	25		
	Create a three-dimensional timeline for the 10 most significant events in your state's history.	25		
	Select an important person in your state's history and write a journal that the person may have kept during his or her lifetime.	25		
	Create a quiz board to test your classmates' knowledge about the important people in your state's history.	25		
	Total number of points you are planning to earn from Side 1.		**Total points earned from Side 1:**	

Our State's History: Side 2

Plan to Do	Activity to Complete (Side 2: 30 points and up)	Point Value	Date Completed	Points Earned
	Choose the leader who you feel made the biggest difference in where your state is today. Present a You Be the Person presentation in which you come to school as this person and talk about your impact on our state.	30		
	Produce a class lesson on your state and its impact on the history of the states surrounding it.	30		
	Create a class game that allows your classmates to show their knowledge of the geography and history of your state.	35		
	Design a WebQuest that details significant points of interest in your state that are associated with key historical events.	35		
	Design and conduct a survey that asks for opinions about points of interest or historical events. Present your data to your classmates.	35		
	Select someone in your community who is an expert in your state's history. Interview this person and make a poster to show what you learned.	40		
	The President of the National Museum is adding a whole wing of state exhibits. These exhibits have to include information on a state's history, its leaders, and its historical locations. Create a museum exhibit that will represent your state well!	50		
	Free choice: must be outlined on a proposal form and approved before beginning work.	10–40 points		
	Total number of points you are planning to earn from Side 1.	**Total points earned from Side 1:**		
	Total number of points you are planning to earn from Side 2.	**Total points earned from Side 2:**		
		Grand Total (/100)		

I am planning to complete ـــــ activities that could earn up to a total of ـــــــ points.

Teacher's initials ـــــــــ Student's signature _____

Name:_____ Date:_____ ●

Our State's History: Side 1

Guidelines:
1. You may complete as many of the activities listed as you can within the time period.
2. You may choose any combination of activities.
3. Your goal is 100 points. You may earn up to _____ points extra credit.
4. You may be as creative as you like within the guidelines listed below.
5. You must show your plan to your teacher by _____.
6. Activities may be turned in at any time during the working time period. They will be graded and recorded on this sheet as you continue to work, so keep it safe!

Plan to Do	Activity to Complete (Side 1: 10–25 points)	Point Value	Date Completed	Points Earned
	Complete another student's crossword puzzle.	10		
	Create a collage that shares photos, words, and important information about your state and its history.	15		
	Create a crossword puzzle about your state's history.	15		
	Make a flipbook of the important events in your state's history.	15		
	Create a diorama of your state's most important historical location. Include a paragraph about why this location is the most important.	20		
	Design a folded flipbook for your state's history and its leaders throughout its history.	20		
	Create a quiz board to test your classmates' knowledge about the important people in your state's history.	20		
	Select an important person in your state's history and write a journal that the person may have kept during his or her lifetime.	25		
	Create a PowerPoint presentation that provides information about the location you feel is most important in your state.	25		
	Create a three-dimensional timeline for the 10 most significant events in your state's history.	25		
	Design a book cover for a book about your state's history.	25		
	Design an advertisement for one of your state's historical locations.	25		
	Total number of points you are planning to earn from Side 1.	**Total points earned from Side 1:**		

Name:_____ Date:_____

Our State's History: Side 2

Plan to Do	Activity to Complete (Side 2: 30 points and up)	Point Value	Date Completed	Points Earned
	Create a class game that allows your classmates to show their knowledge of the geography and history of your state.	30		
	Choose the leader who you feel made the biggest difference in where your state is today. Present a You Be the Person presentation in which you come to school as this person and talk about your impact on our state.	30		
	Design a WebQuest that details significant points of interest in your state that are associated with key historical events.	30		
	Produce a class lesson on your state and its impact on the history of the states surrounding it.	30		
	Design and conduct a survey that asks for opinions about points of interest or historical events. Present your data to your classmates.	35		
	Select someone in your community who is an expert in your state's history. Interview this person and make a poster to show what you learned.	40		
	The President of the National Museum is adding a whole wing of state exhibits. These exhibits have to include information on a state's history, its leaders and its historical locations. Create a museum exhibit that will represent your state well!	50		
	Free choice: must be outlined on a proposal form and approved before beginning work.	10–40 points		
	Total number of points you are planning to earn from Side 1.	**Total points earned from Side 1:**		
	Total number of points you are planning to earn from Side 2.	**Total points earned from Side 2:**		
		Grand Total (/100)		

I am planning to complete _____ activities that could earn up to a total of _____ points.

Teacher's initials _____ Student's signature _____

Resources

Aron, P. (1998). *Unsolved mysteries of American history: An eye-opening journey through 500 years of discoveries, disappearances, and baffling events.* New York, NY: John Wiley & Sons.

Beyer, R. (2003). *The greatest stories never told: 100 tales from history to astonish, bewilder, and stupefy.* New York, NY: HarperCollins.

Escobar, D. (2001). *Creating history documentaries.* Waco, TX; Prufrock Press.

Freedman, R. (1995). *Immigrant kids.* New York, NY: Puffin Books.

Lindquist, T., & Selwyn, D. (2000). *Social studies at the center: Integrating kids, content and literacy.* Portsmouth, NH: Heinemann.

Lindquist, T. (2002). *Seeing the whole through social studies* (2nd ed.). Portsmouth, NH: Heinemann.

Loewen, J. W. (2008). *Lies my teacher told me: Everything your American history textbook got wrong* (Rev. ed.). New York, NY: Touchstone.

Obenchain, K. M., & Morris, R. V. (2006). *50 social studies strategies for K–8 classrooms* (2nd ed.). Chicago, IL: Prentice Hall.

Ouzts, S. B. (2000). *Social studies projects for the gifted student.* New York, NY: Good Apple.

Selwyn, D. (1993). *Living history in the classroom.* Waco, TX; Prufrock Press.

References

Anderson, L., & Krathwohl, D. (Eds.). (2001). *A taxonomy for learning, teaching, and assessing: A revision of Bloom's taxonomy for educational objectives* (Complete ed.). New York, NY: Longman.

Mercer, C. D., Lane, H. B., Jordan, L., Allsopp, D. H., & Eisele, M. R. (1996). Empowering teachers and students with instructional choices in inclusive settings. *Remedial & Special Education, 17,* 226–236.

About the Author

After teaching science for more than 15 years, both overseas and in the U.S., **Laurie E. Westphal** now works as an independent gifted education and science consultant nationwide. She enjoys developing and presenting staff development on differentiation for various districts and conferences, working with teachers to assist them in planning and developing lessons to meet the needs of all students. Laurie currently resides in Houston, TX, and has made it her goal to convert as many teachers as she can to the differentiated lifestyle in the classroom and share her vision for real-world, product-based lessons that help all students become critical thinkers and effective problem solvers.

If you are interested in having Laurie speak at your next staff development day or conference, please visit her website, http://www.giftedconsultant.com, for additional information.

Additional Titles by the Author

Laurie E. Westphal has written many books on using differentiation strategies in the classroom, providing teachers of grades K–8 with creative, engaging, ready-to-use resources. Among them are:

Differentiating Instruction With Menus, Grades K–2
(Math, Language Arts, Science, and Social Studies volumes available)

Differentiating Instruction With Menus, Grades 3–5
(Math, Language Arts, Science, and Social Studies volumes available)

Differentiating Instruction With Menus, Grades 6–8
(Math, Language Arts, Science, and Social Studies volumes available)

Differentiating Instruction With Menus for the Inclusive Classroom, Grades K–2
(Math, Language Arts, Science, and Social Studies volumes available Spring 2013)

Differentiating Instruction With Menus for the Inclusive Classroom, Grades 3–5
(Math, Language Arts, Science, and Social Studies volumes available)

Differentiating Instruction With Menus for the Inclusive Classroom, Grades 6–8
(Math, Language Arts, Science, and Social Studies volumes available)

**For a current listing of Laurie's books, please visit
Prufrock Press at http://www.prufrock.com.**